SUPERHEROES ON A MEDICAL MISSION

"WHAT'S UP WITH PAM?"

MEDIKIDZ EXPLAIN CHILDHOOD OBESITY

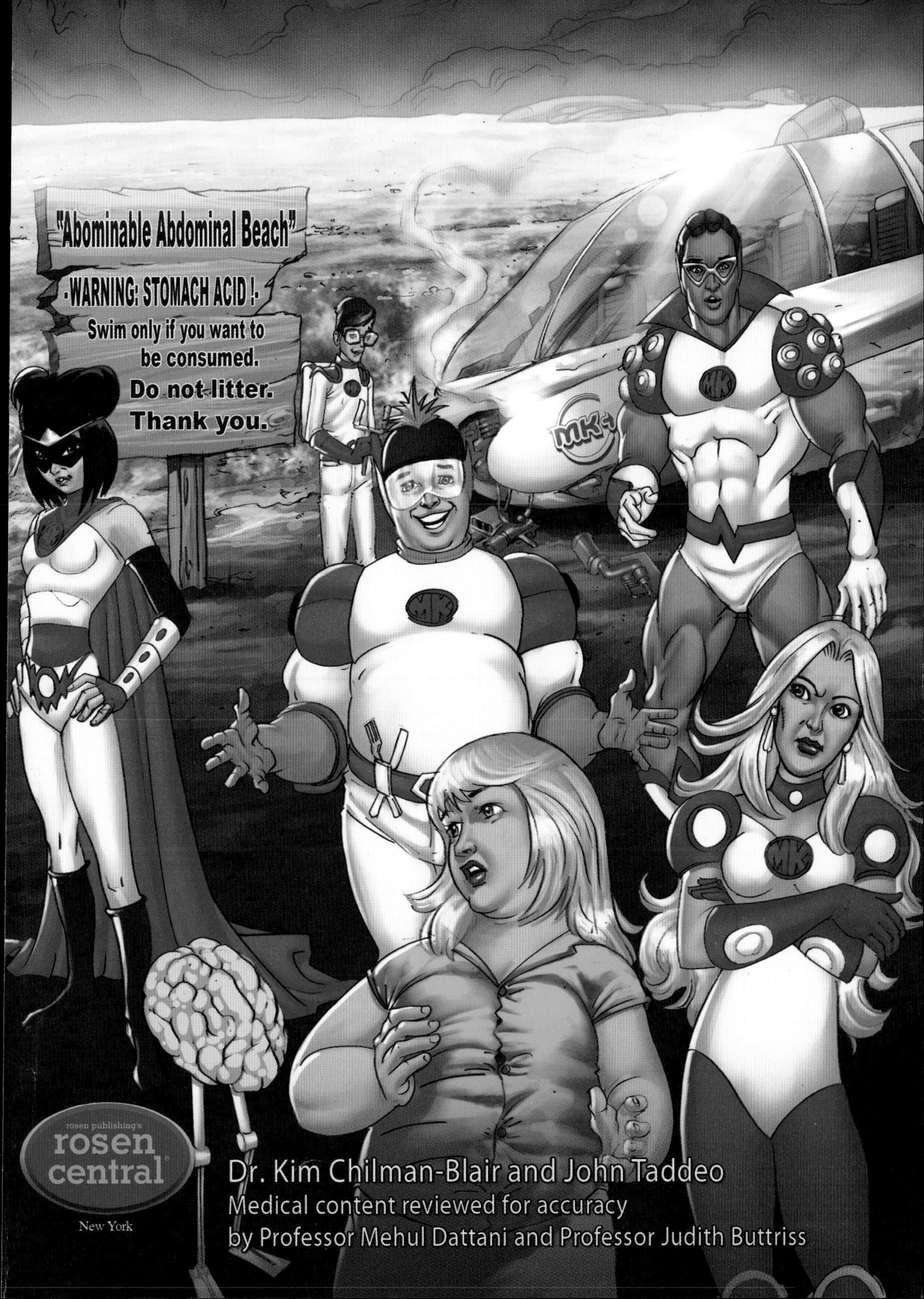

"Abominable Abdominal Beach"
-WARNING: STOMACH ACID !-
Swim only if you want to be consumed.
Do not litter.
Thank you.
MK

rosen publishing's
rosen central
New York

Dr. Kim Chilman-Blair and John Taddeo

Medical content reviewed for accuracy
by Professor Mehul Dattani and Professor Judith Buttriss

This edition published in 2010 by:

The Rosen Publishing Group, Inc.
29 East 21st Street
New York, NY 10010

Library of Congress Cataloging-in-Publication Data

Chilman-Blair, Dr. Kim.
"What's up with Pam?": Medikidz explain childhood obesity / Dr. Kim Chilman-Blair and John Taddeo; medical content reviewed for accuracy by Professor Mehul Dattani and Professor Judith Buttriss.
    p. cm.—(Superheroes on a medical mission)
Includes index.
ISBN 978-1-4358-3535-1 (library binding)
1. Obesity in children—Comic books, strips, etc. I. Taddeo, John. II. Title.
RJ399.C6.C55 2010
618.92'398—dc22

2009026794

Manufactured in China

CPSIA Compliance Information: Batch #MW0102YA: For Further Information contact Rosen Publishing, New York, New York at 1-800-237-9932

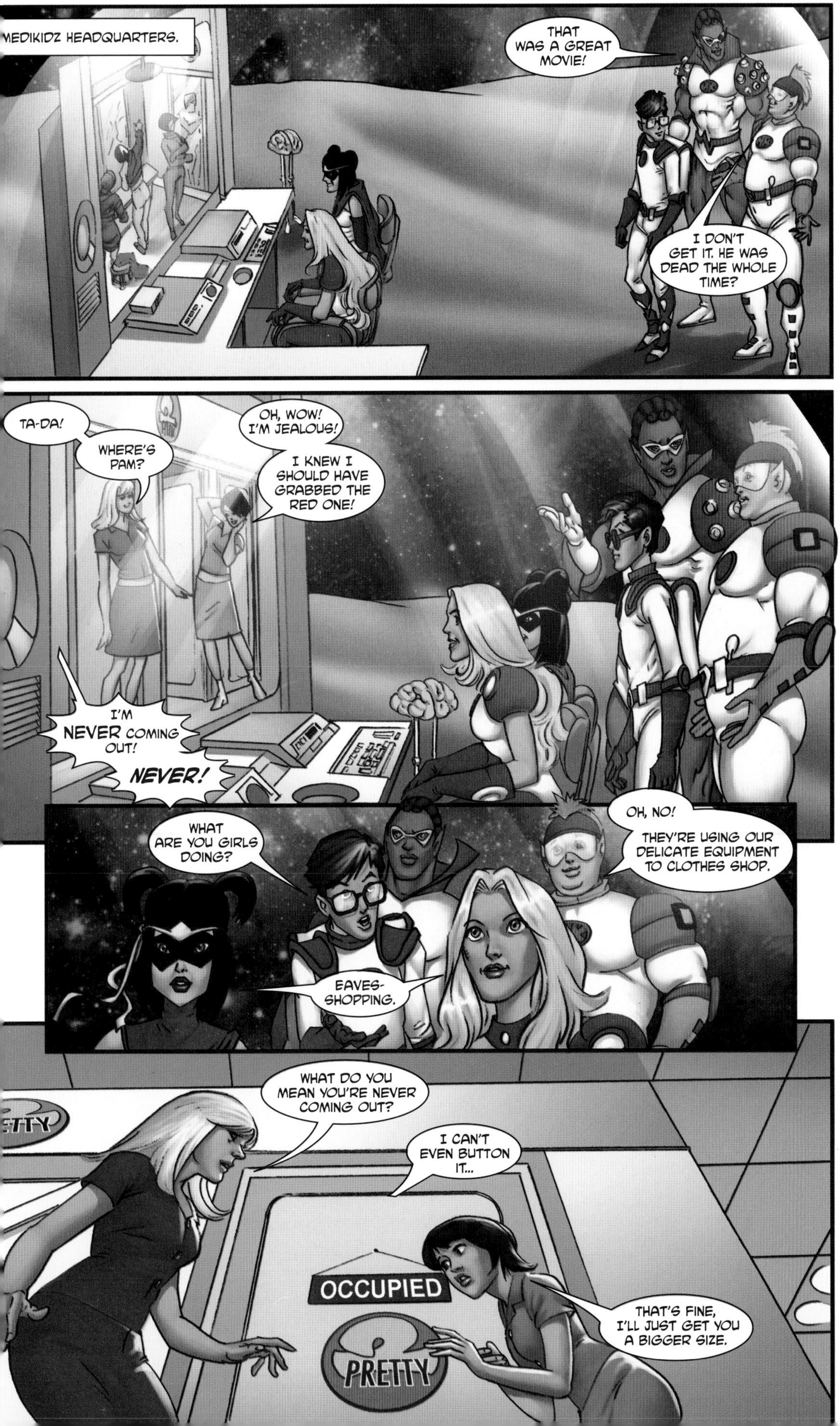
MEDIKIDZ HEADQUARTERS.
THAT WAS A GREAT MOVIE!
I DON'T GET IT. HE WAS DEAD THE WHOLE TIME?
TA-DA!
WHERE'S PAM?
OH, WOW! I'M JEALOUS!
I KNEW I SHOULD HAVE GRABBED THE RED ONE!
I'M NEVER COMING OUT!
NEVER!
WHAT ARE YOU GIRLS DOING?
OH, NO!
THEY'RE USING OUR DELICATE EQUIPMENT TO CLOTHES SHOP.
EAVES-SHOPPING.
PRETTY
WHAT DO YOU MEAN YOU'RE NEVER COMING OUT?
I CAN'T EVEN BUTTON IT...
OCCUPIED
PRETTY
THAT'S FINE, I'LL JUST GET YOU A BIGGER SIZE.

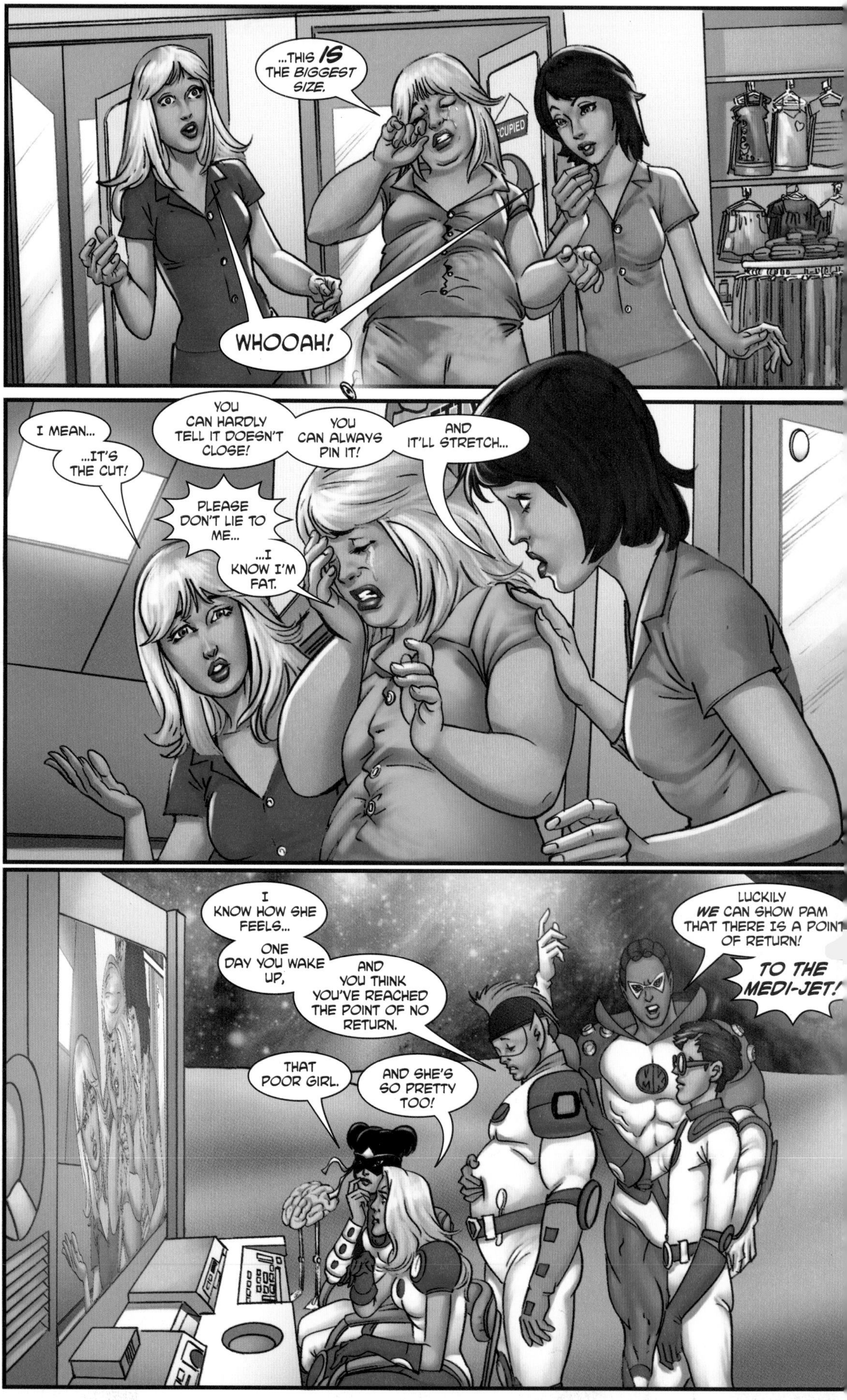
...THIS IS THE BIGGEST SIZE.
OCCUPIED
WHOOAH!
I MEAN...
...IT'S THE CUT!
YOU CAN HARDLY TELL IT DOESN'T CLOSE!
YOU CAN ALWAYS PIN IT!
AND IT'LL STRETCH...
PLEASE DON'T LIE TO ME...
...I KNOW I'M FAT.
I KNOW HOW SHE FEELS...
ONE DAY YOU WAKE UP,
AND YOU THINK YOU'VE REACHED THE POINT OF NO RETURN.
THAT POOR GIRL.
AND SHE'S SO PRETTY TOO!
LUCKILY WE CAN SHOW PAM THAT THERE IS A POINT OF RETURN!
TO THE MEDI-JET!

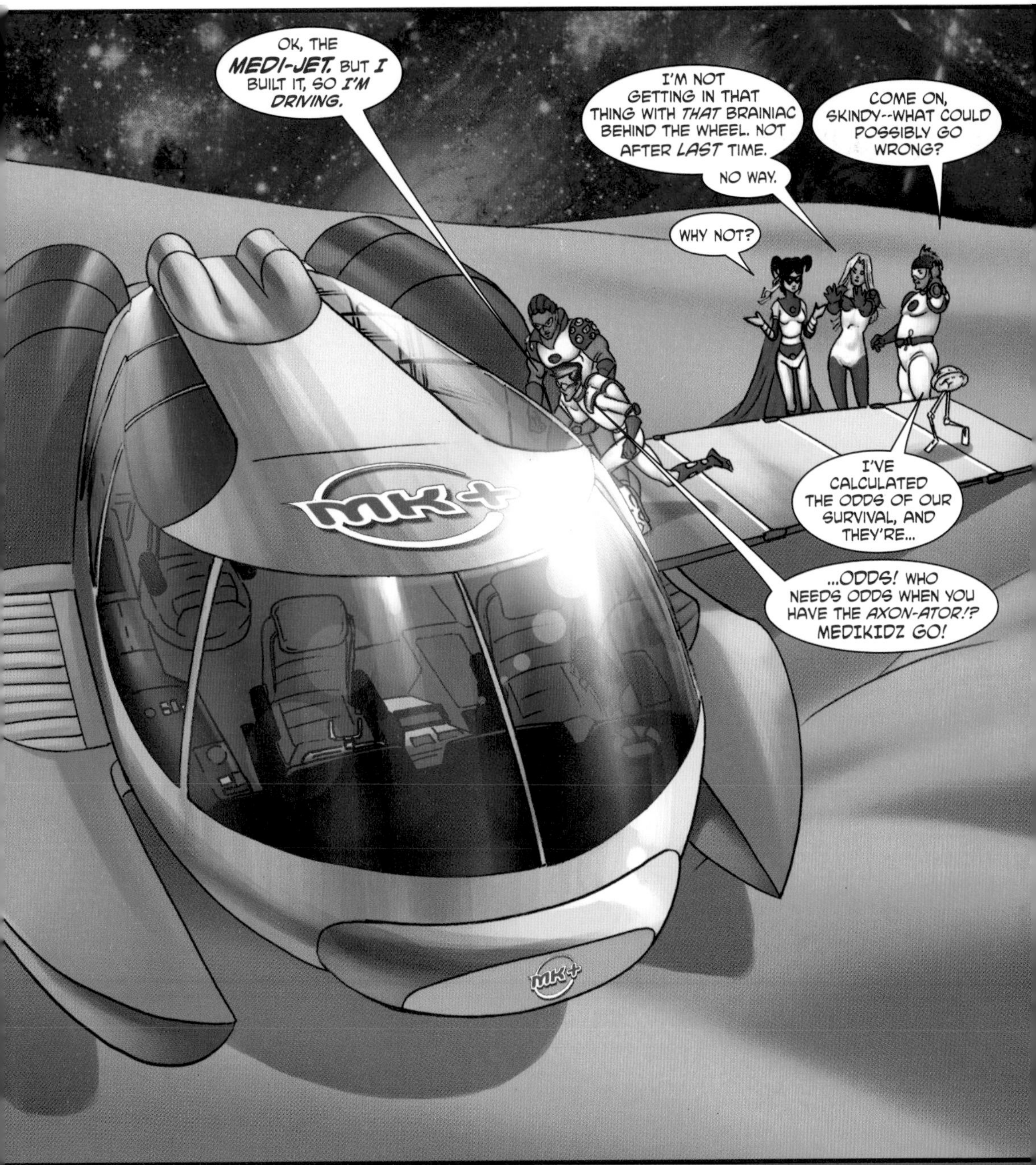
OK, THE MEDI-JET. BUT I BUILT IT, SO I'M DRIVING.
WHY NOT?
I'M NOT GETTING IN THAT THING WITH THAT BRAINIAC BEHIND THE WHEEL. NOT AFTER LAST TIME.
NO WAY.
COME ON, SKINDY--WHAT COULD POSSIBLY GO WRONG?
I'VE CALCULATED THE ODDS OF OUR SURVIVAL, AND THEY'RE...
...ODDS! WHO NEEDS ODDS WHEN YOU HAVE THE AXON-ATOR!? MEDIKIDZ GO!
MK+
MK+

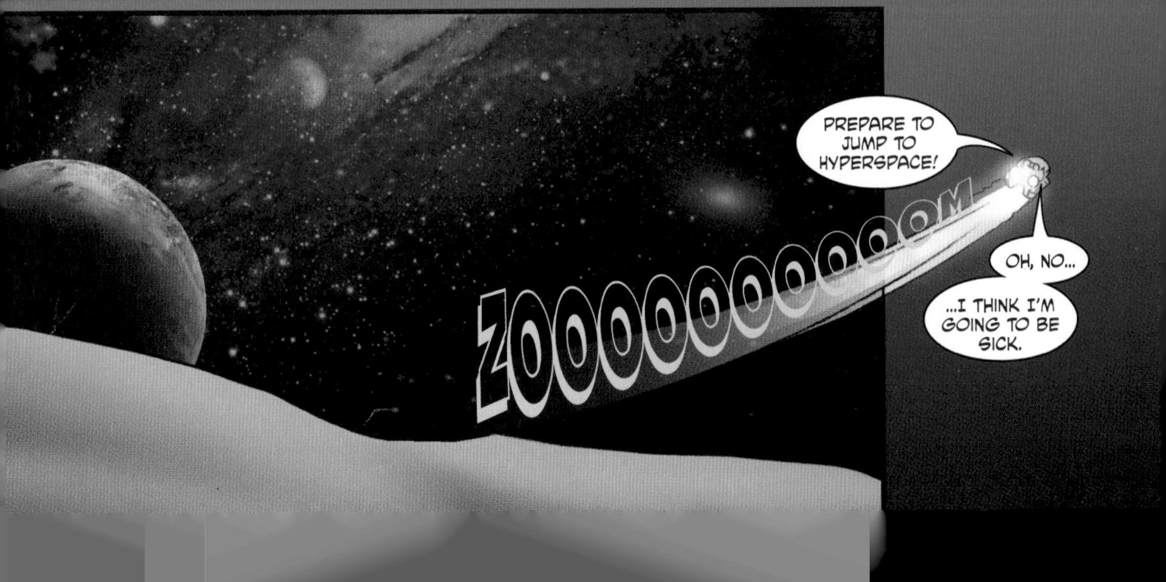
PREPARE TO JUMP TO HYPERSPACE!
ZOOOOOOOOOOOOM
OH, NO...
...I THINK I'M GOING TO BE SICK.

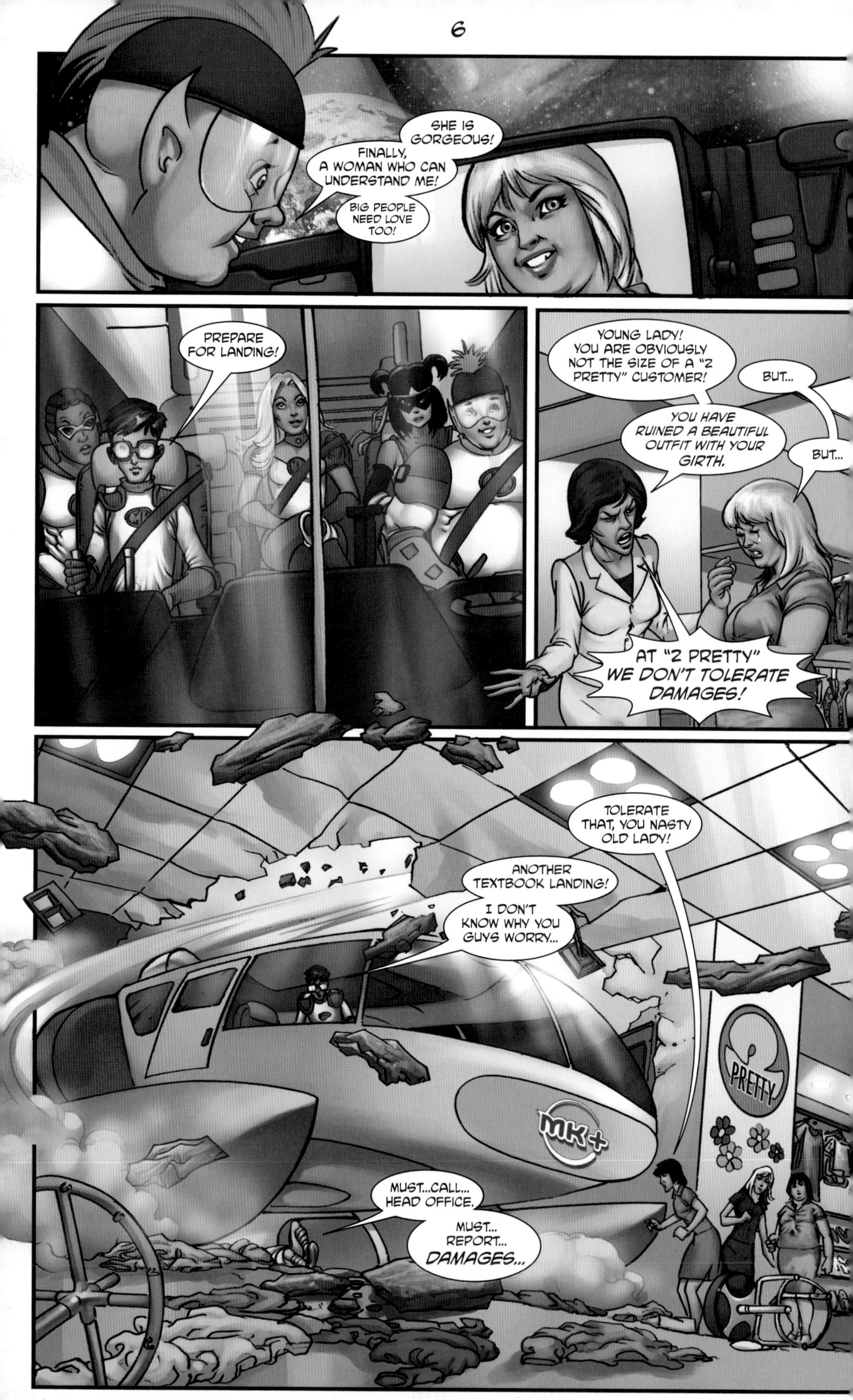
SHE IS GORGEOUS!
FINALLY, A WOMAN WHO CAN UNDERSTAND ME!
BIG PEOPLE NEED LOVE TOO!
PREPARE FOR LANDING!
YOUNG LADY! YOU ARE OBVIOUSLY NOT THE SIZE OF A "2 PRETTY" CUSTOMER!
BUT...
YOU HAVE RUINED A BEAUTIFUL OUTFIT WITH YOUR GIRTH.
BUT...
AT "2 PRETTY" WE DON'T TOLERATE DAMAGES!
TOLERATE THAT, YOU NASTY OLD LADY!
ANOTHER TEXTBOOK LANDING!
I DON'T KNOW WHY YOU GUYS WORRY...
PRETTY
MK+
MUST...CALL... HEAD OFFICE.
MUST... REPORT... DAMAGES...

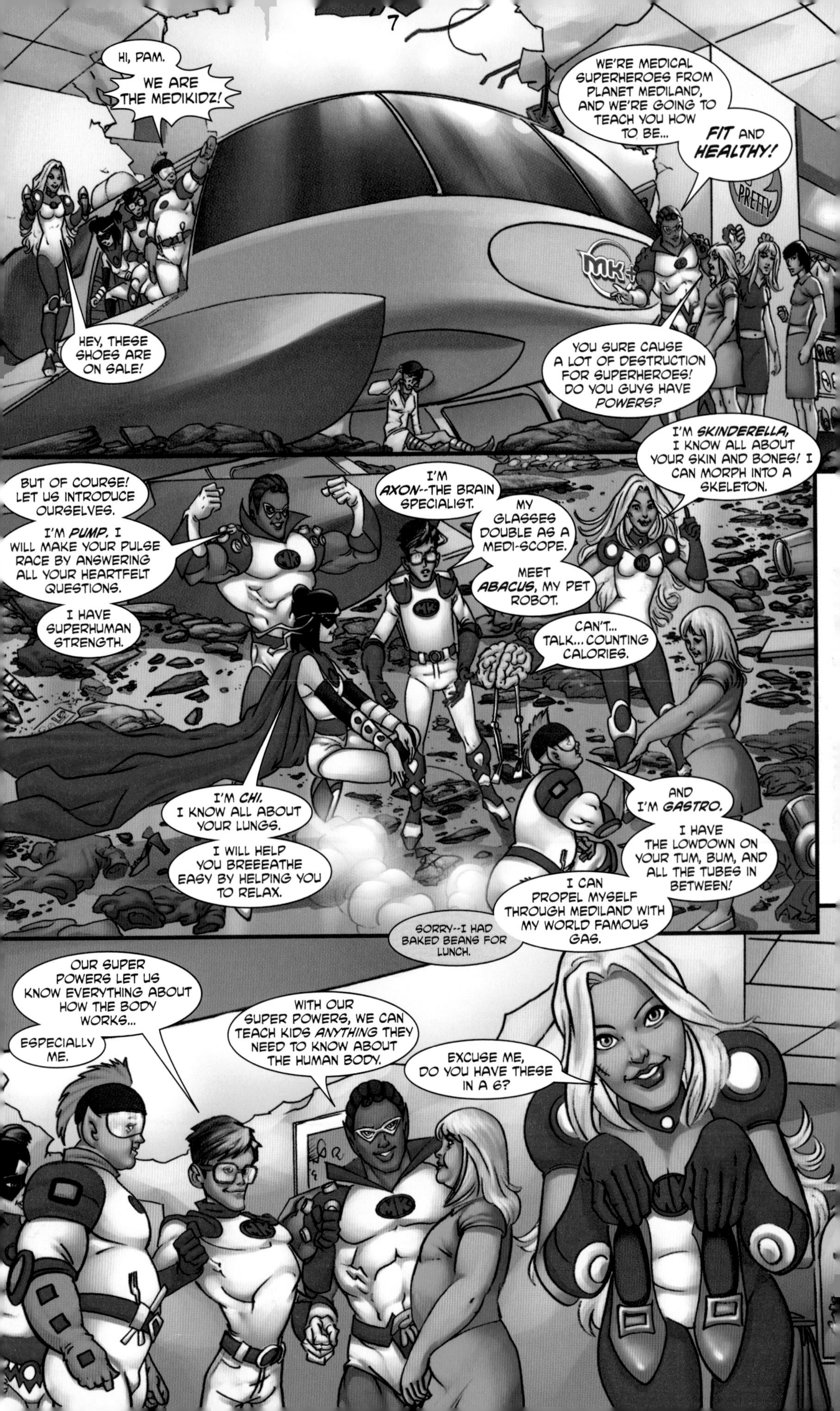

HI, PAM.
WE ARE THE MEDIKIDZ!
WE'RE MEDICAL SUPERHEROES FROM PLANET MEDILAND, AND WE'RE GOING TO TEACH YOU HOW TO BE... FIT AND HEALTHY!
PRETTY
MK+
HEY, THESE SHOES ARE ON SALE!
YOU SURE CAUSE A LOT OF DESTRUCTION FOR SUPERHEROES! DO YOU GUYS HAVE POWERS?
BUT OF COURSE! LET US INTRODUCE OURSELVES.
I'M PUMP. I WILL MAKE YOUR PULSE RACE BY ANSWERING ALL YOUR HEARTFELT QUESTIONS.
I HAVE SUPERHUMAN STRENGTH.
I'M AXON--THE BRAIN SPECIALIST.
MY GLASSES DOUBLE AS A MEDI-SCOPE.
MEET ABACUS, MY PET ROBOT.
I'M SKINDERELLA, I KNOW ALL ABOUT YOUR SKIN AND BONES! I CAN MORPH INTO A SKELETON.
CAN'T... TALK... COUNTING CALORIES.
I'M CHI. I KNOW ALL ABOUT YOUR LUNGS.
I WILL HELP YOU BREEEATHE EASY BY HELPING YOU TO RELAX.
AND I'M GASTRO.
I HAVE THE LOWDOWN ON YOUR TUM, BUM, AND ALL THE TUBES IN BETWEEN!
I CAN PROPEL MYSELF THROUGH MEDILAND WITH MY WORLD FAMOUS GAS.
SORRY--I HAD BAKED BEANS FOR LUNCH.
OUR SUPER POWERS LET US KNOW EVERYTHING ABOUT HOW THE BODY WORKS...
ESPECIALLY ME.
WITH OUR SUPER POWERS, WE CAN TEACH KIDS ANYTHING THEY NEED TO KNOW ABOUT THE HUMAN BODY.
EXCUSE ME, DO YOU HAVE THESE IN A 6?

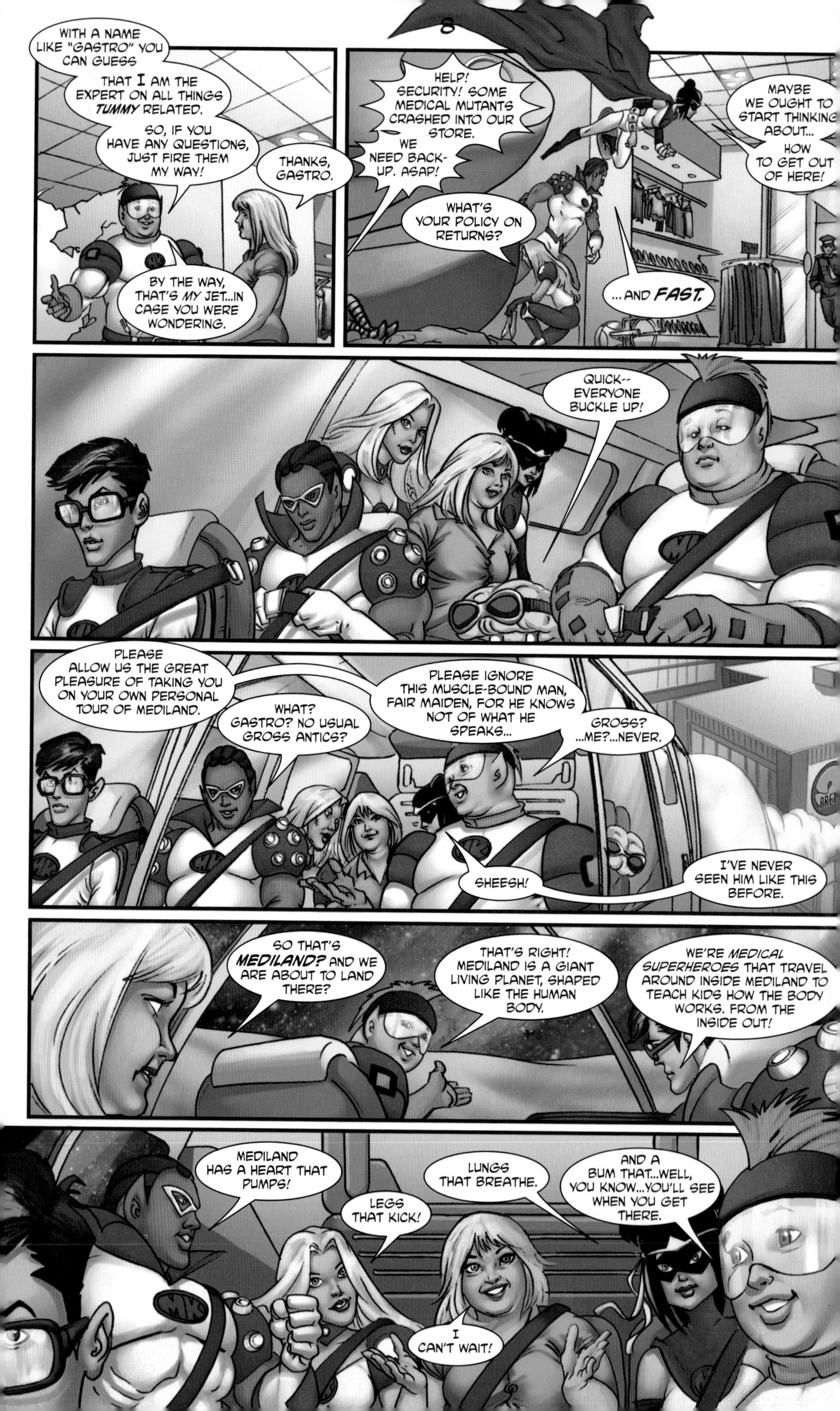
WITH A NAME LIKE "GASTRO" YOU CAN GUESS
THAT I AM THE EXPERT ON ALL THINGS TUMMY RELATED.
SO, IF YOU HAVE ANY QUESTIONS, JUST FIRE THEM MY WAY!
THANKS, GASTRO.
BY THE WAY, THAT'S MY JET...IN CASE YOU WERE WONDERING.
HELP! SECURITY! SOME MEDICAL MUTANTS CRASHED INTO OUR STORE.
WE NEED BACK-UP. ASAP!
WHAT'S YOUR POLICY ON RETURNS?
MAYBE WE OUGHT TO START THINKING ABOUT...
HOW TO GET OUT OF HERE!
...AND FAST.
QUICK-- EVERYONE BUCKLE UP!
PLEASE ALLOW US THE GREAT PLEASURE OF TAKING YOU ON YOUR OWN PERSONAL TOUR OF MEDILAND.
PLEASE IGNORE THIS MUSCLE-BOUND MAN, FAIR MAIDEN, FOR HE KNOWS NOT OF WHAT HE SPEAKS...
WHAT? GASTRO? NO USUAL GROSS ANTICS?
GROSS? ...ME?...NEVER.
SHEESH!
I'VE NEVER SEEN HIM LIKE THIS BEFORE.
SO THAT'S MEDILAND? AND WE ARE ABOUT TO LAND THERE?
THAT'S RIGHT! MEDILAND IS A GIANT LIVING PLANET, SHAPED LIKE THE HUMAN BODY.
WE'RE MEDICAL SUPERHEROES THAT TRAVEL AROUND INSIDE MEDILAND TO TEACH KIDS HOW THE BODY WORKS. FROM THE INSIDE OUT!
MEDILAND HAS A HEART THAT PUMPS!
LEGS THAT KICK!
LUNGS THAT BREATHE.
AND A BUM THAT...WELL, YOU KNOW...YOU'LL SEE WHEN YOU GET THERE.
I CAN'T WAIT!

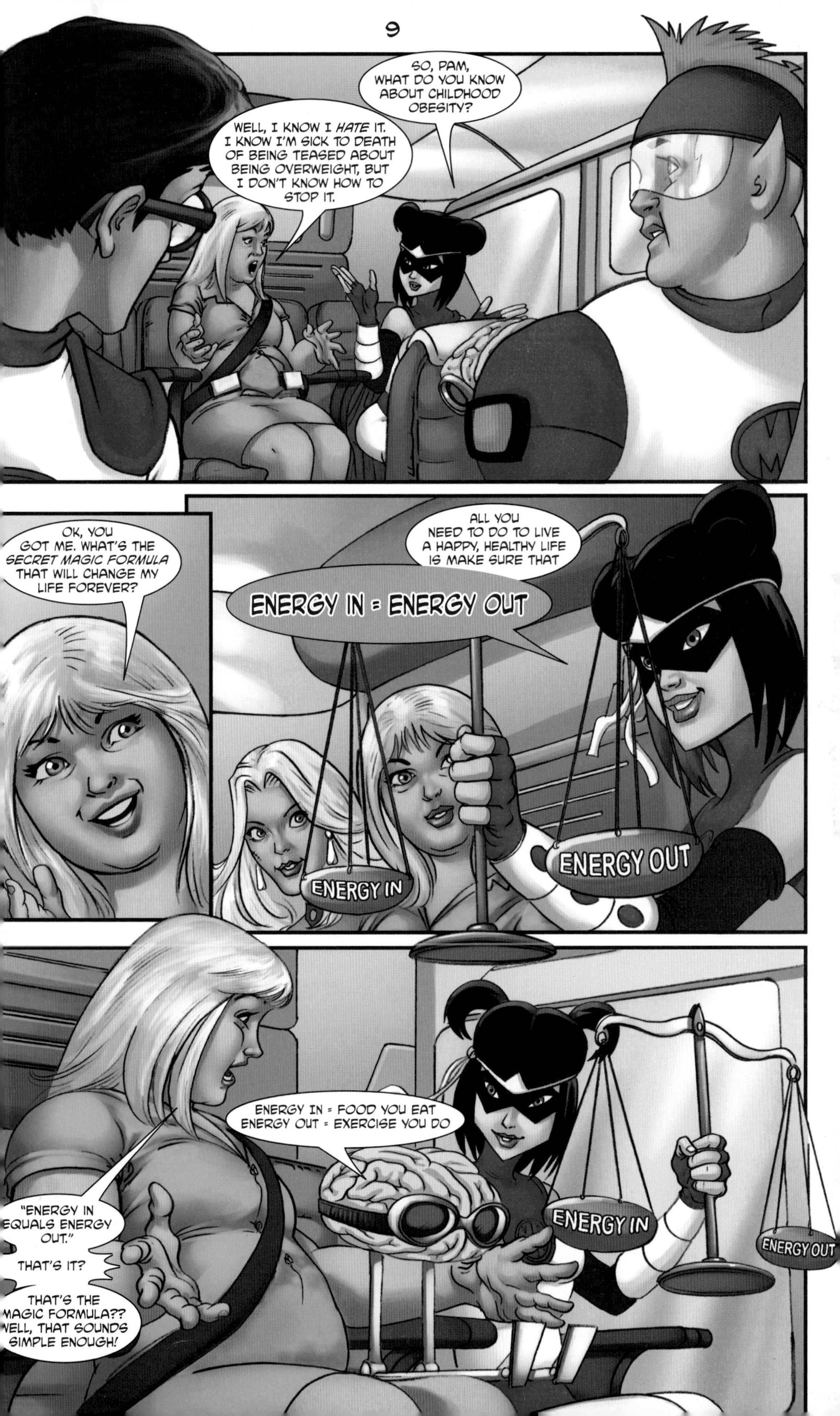
SO, PAM, WHAT DO YOU KNOW ABOUT CHILDHOOD OBESITY?
WELL, I KNOW I *HATE* IT. I KNOW I'M SICK TO DEATH OF BEING TEASED ABOUT BEING OVERWEIGHT, BUT I DON'T KNOW HOW TO STOP IT.
OK, YOU GOT ME. WHAT'S THE *SECRET MAGIC FORMULA* THAT WILL CHANGE MY LIFE FOREVER?
ALL YOU NEED TO DO TO LIVE A HAPPY, HEALTHY LIFE IS MAKE SURE THAT
ENERGY IN = ENERGY OUT
ENERGY IN
ENERGY OUT
ENERGY IN = FOOD YOU EAT
ENERGY OUT = EXERCISE YOU DO
"ENERGY IN EQUALS ENERGY OUT."
THAT'S IT?
THAT'S THE MAGIC FORMULA?? WELL, THAT SOUNDS SIMPLE ENOUGH!
ENERGY IN
ENERGY OUT

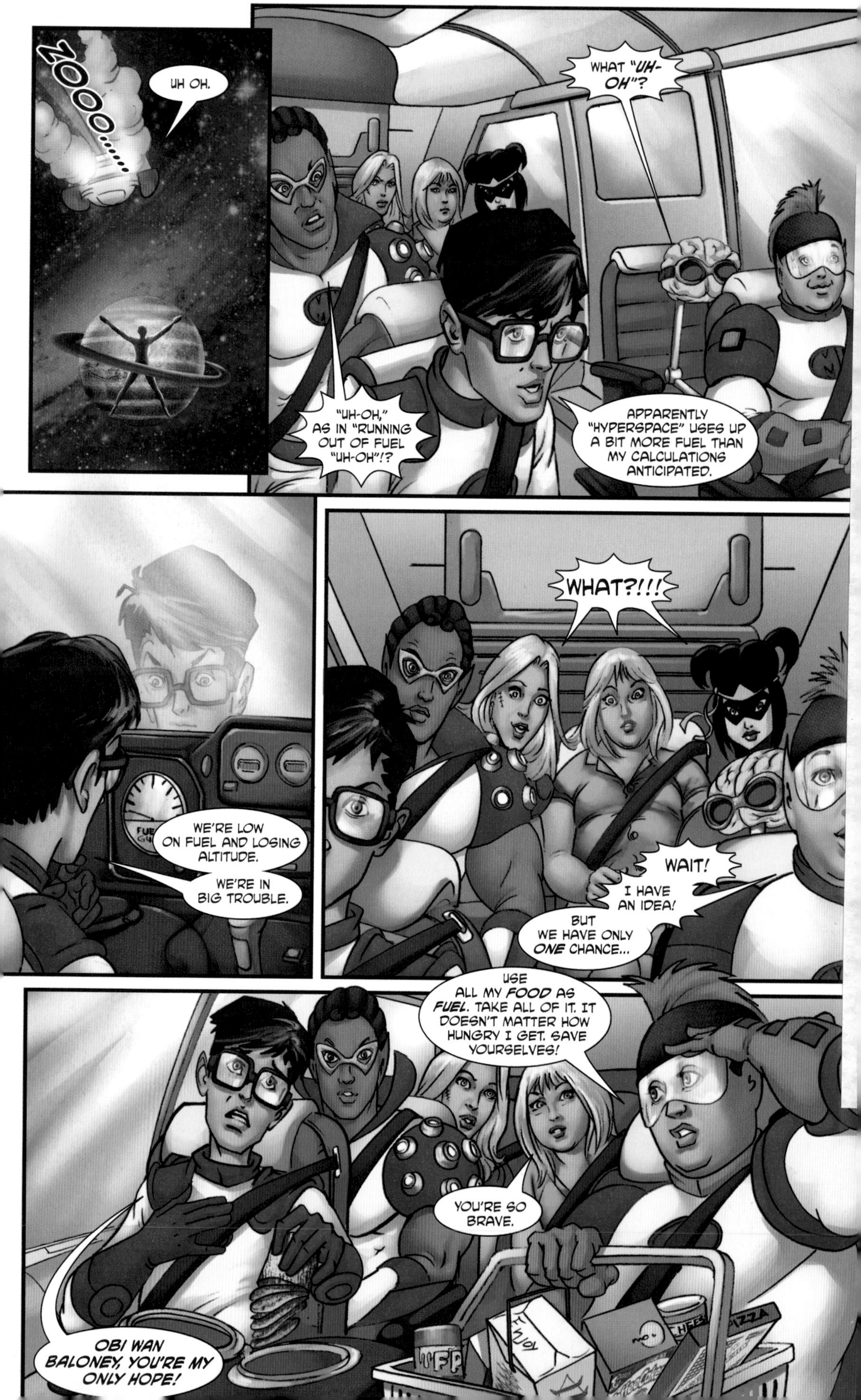
ZOOO.....
UH OH.
WHAT "UH-OH"?
"UH-OH," AS IN "RUNNING OUT OF FUEL "UH-OH"!?
APPARENTLY "HYPERSPACE" USES UP A BIT MORE FUEL THAN MY CALCULATIONS ANTICIPATED.
WE'RE LOW ON FUEL AND LOSING ALTITUDE.
WE'RE IN BIG TROUBLE.
WHAT?!!!
WAIT!
I HAVE AN IDEA!
BUT WE HAVE ONLY ONE CHANCE...
USE ALL MY FOOD AS FUEL. TAKE ALL OF IT. IT DOESN'T MATTER HOW HUNGRY I GET. SAVE YOURSELVES!
YOU'RE SO BRAVE.
OBI WAN BALONEY, YOU'RE MY ONLY HOPE!

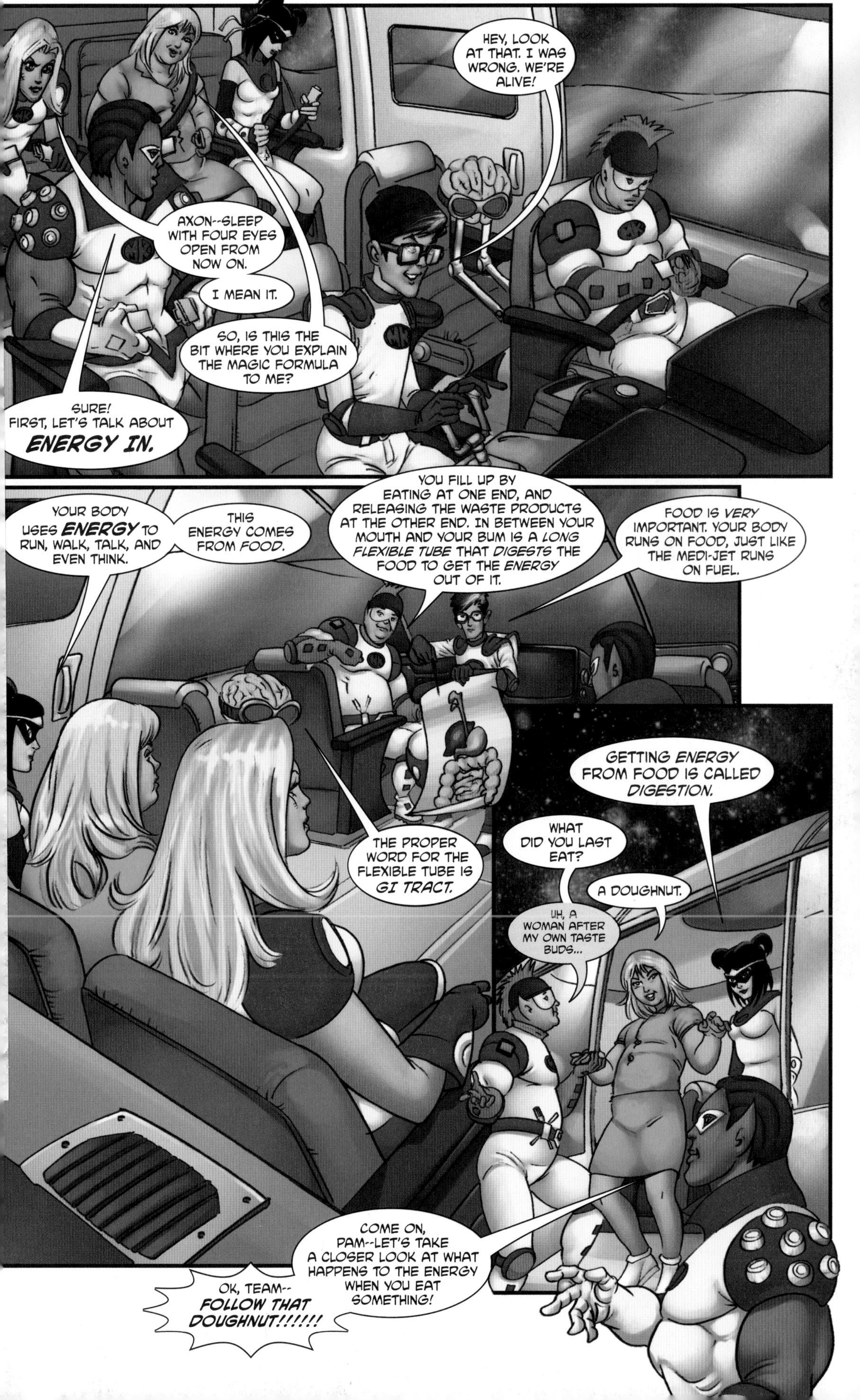
HEY, LOOK AT THAT. I WAS WRONG. WE'RE ALIVE!
AXON--SLEEP WITH FOUR EYES OPEN FROM NOW ON.
I MEAN IT.
SO, IS THIS THE BIT WHERE YOU EXPLAIN THE MAGIC FORMULA TO ME?
SURE! FIRST, LET'S TALK ABOUT ENERGY IN.
YOUR BODY USES ENERGY TO RUN, WALK, TALK, AND EVEN THINK.
THIS ENERGY COMES FROM FOOD.
YOU FILL UP BY EATING AT ONE END, AND RELEASING THE WASTE PRODUCTS AT THE OTHER END. IN BETWEEN YOUR MOUTH AND YOUR BUM IS A LONG FLEXIBLE TUBE THAT DIGESTS THE FOOD TO GET THE ENERGY OUT OF IT.
FOOD IS VERY IMPORTANT. YOUR BODY RUNS ON FOOD, JUST LIKE THE MEDI-JET RUNS ON FUEL.
THE PROPER WORD FOR THE FLEXIBLE TUBE IS GI TRACT.
GETTING ENERGY FROM FOOD IS CALLED DIGESTION.
WHAT DID YOU LAST EAT?
A DOUGHNUT.
UH, A WOMAN AFTER MY OWN TASTE BUDS...
COME ON, PAM--LET'S TAKE A CLOSER LOOK AT WHAT HAPPENS TO THE ENERGY WHEN YOU EAT SOMETHING!
OK, TEAM-- FOLLOW THAT DOUGHNUT!!!!!!

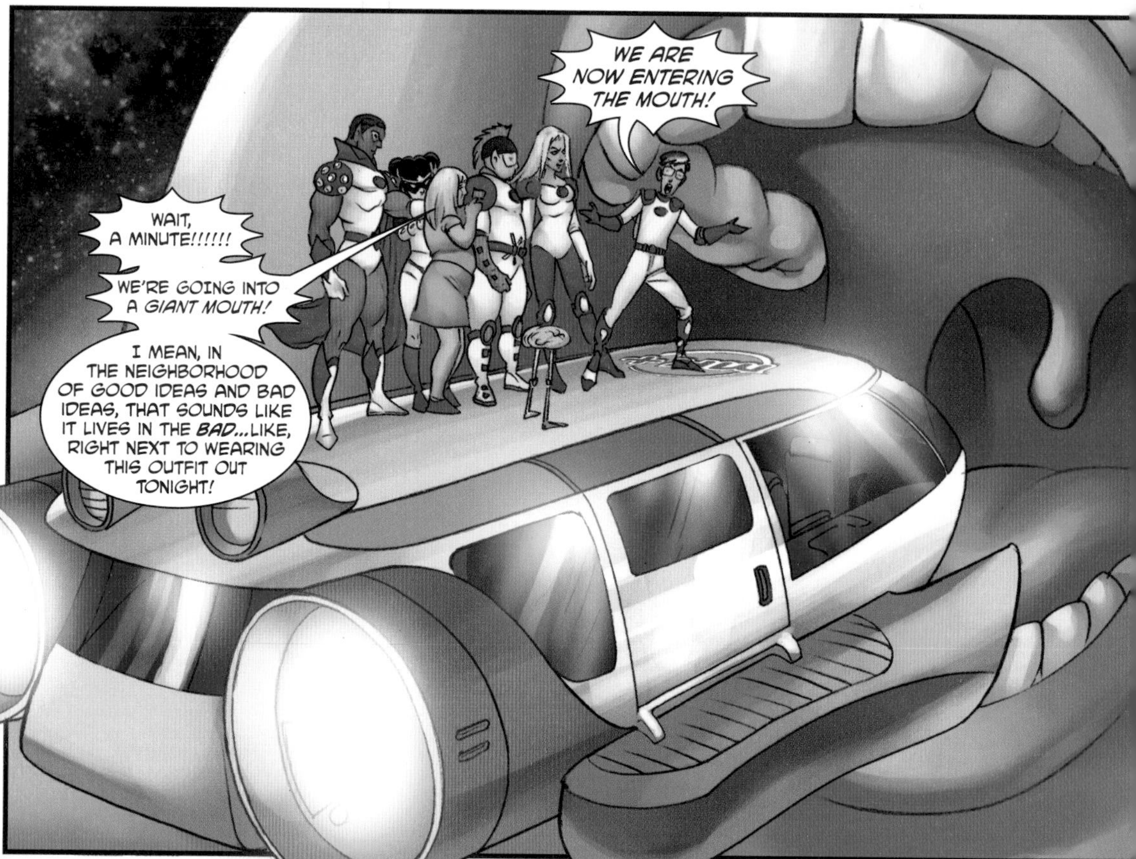
WE ARE NOW ENTERING THE MOUTH!
WAIT, A MINUTE!!!!!!
WE'RE GOING INTO A *GIANT MOUTH!*
I MEAN, IN THE NEIGHBORHOOD OF GOOD IDEAS AND BAD IDEAS, THAT SOUNDS LIKE IT LIVES IN THE *BAD*...LIKE, RIGHT NEXT TO WEARING THIS OUTFIT OUT TONIGHT!

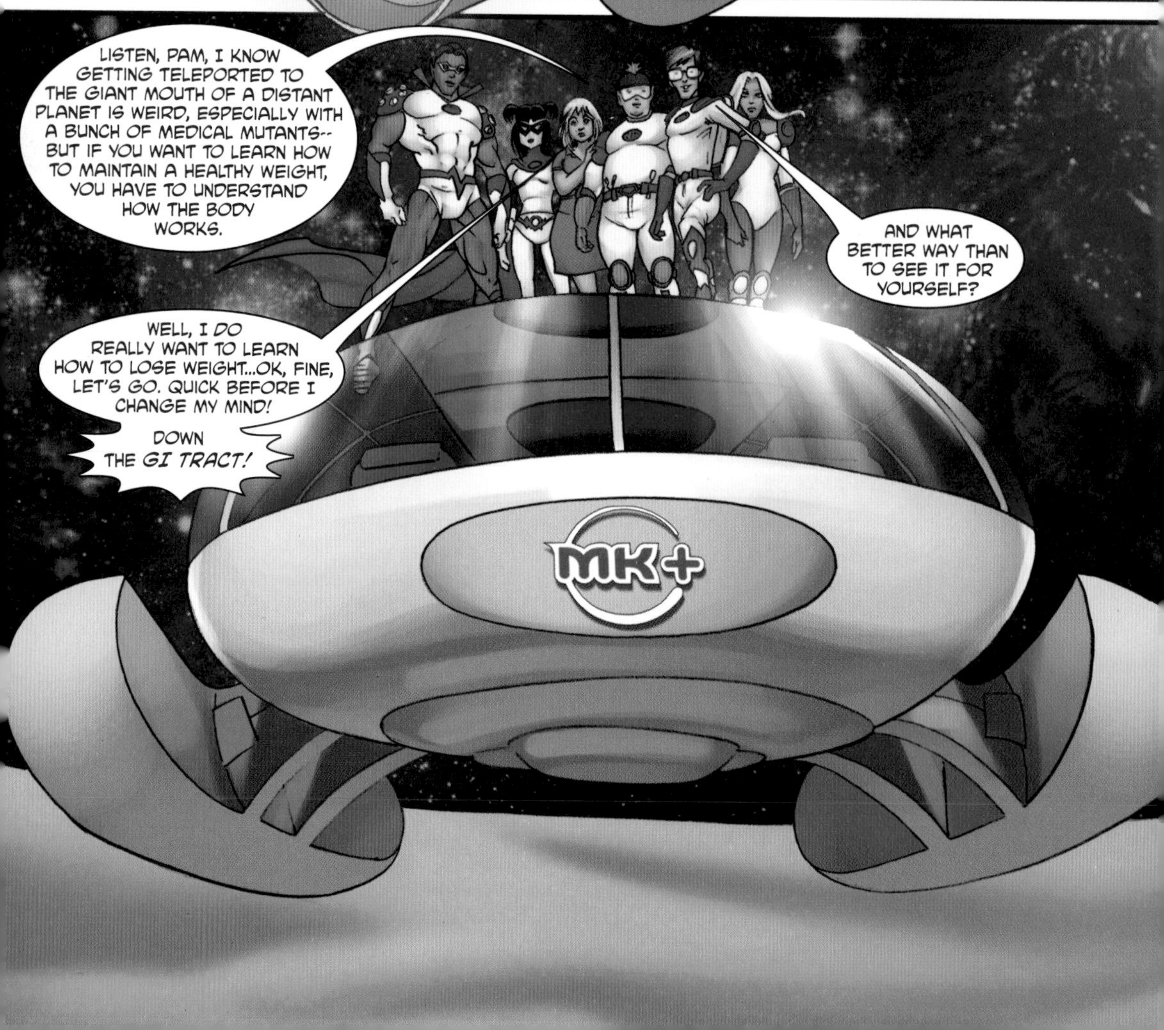
LISTEN, PAM, I KNOW GETTING TELEPORTED TO THE GIANT MOUTH OF A DISTANT PLANET IS WEIRD, ESPECIALLY WITH A BUNCH OF MEDICAL MUTANTS-- BUT IF YOU WANT TO LEARN HOW TO MAINTAIN A HEALTHY WEIGHT, YOU HAVE TO UNDERSTAND HOW THE BODY WORKS.
AND WHAT BETTER WAY THAN TO SEE IT FOR YOURSELF?
WELL, I *DO* REALLY WANT TO LEARN HOW TO LOSE WEIGHT...OK, FINE, LET'S GO. QUICK BEFORE I CHANGE MY MIND!
DOWN THE *GI TRACT!*
MK+

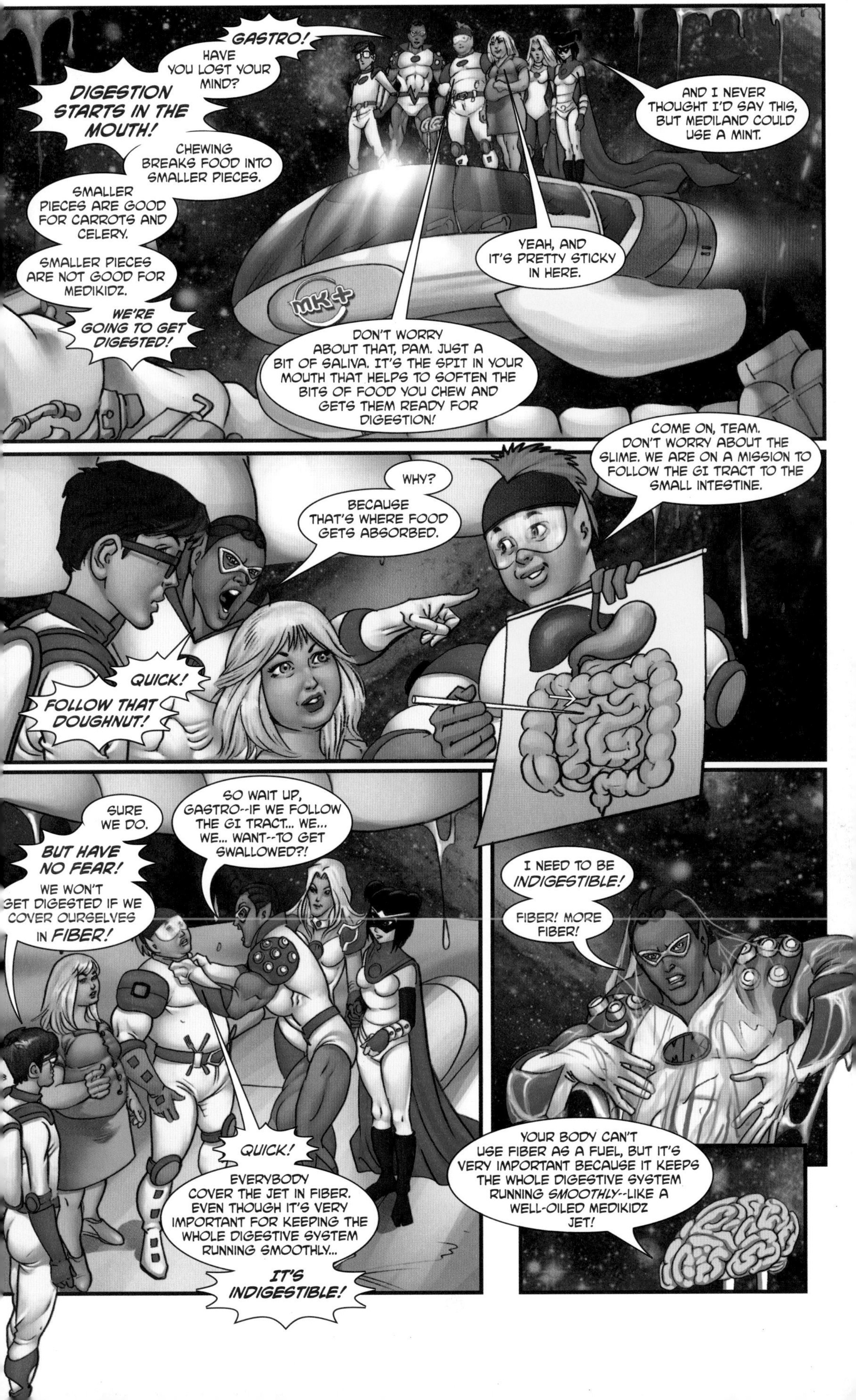
GASTRO!
HAVE YOU LOST YOUR MIND?
DIGESTION STARTS IN THE MOUTH!
CHEWING BREAKS FOOD INTO SMALLER PIECES.
SMALLER PIECES ARE GOOD FOR CARROTS AND CELERY.
SMALLER PIECES ARE NOT GOOD FOR MEDIKIDZ.
WE'RE GOING TO GET DIGESTED!
AND I NEVER THOUGHT I'D SAY THIS, BUT MEDILAND COULD USE A MINT.
YEAH, AND IT'S PRETTY STICKY IN HERE.
MK+
DON'T WORRY ABOUT THAT, PAM. JUST A BIT OF SALIVA. IT'S THE SPIT IN YOUR MOUTH THAT HELPS TO SOFTEN THE BITS OF FOOD YOU CHEW AND GETS THEM READY FOR DIGESTION!
COME ON, TEAM. DON'T WORRY ABOUT THE SLIME. WE ARE ON A MISSION TO FOLLOW THE GI TRACT TO THE SMALL INTESTINE.
WHY?
BECAUSE THAT'S WHERE FOOD GETS ABSORBED.
QUICK!
FOLLOW THAT DOUGHNUT!
SURE WE DO.
SO WAIT UP, GASTRO--IF WE FOLLOW THE GI TRACT... WE... WE... WANT--TO GET SWALLOWED?!
BUT HAVE NO FEAR!
WE WON'T GET DIGESTED IF WE COVER OURSELVES IN FIBER!
QUICK!
EVERYBODY COVER THE JET IN FIBER. EVEN THOUGH IT'S VERY IMPORTANT FOR KEEPING THE WHOLE DIGESTIVE SYSTEM RUNNING SMOOTHLY...
IT'S INDIGESTIBLE!
I NEED TO BE INDIGESTIBLE!
FIBER! MORE FIBER!
YOUR BODY CAN'T USE FIBER AS A FUEL, BUT IT'S VERY IMPORTANT BECAUSE IT KEEPS THE WHOLE DIGESTIVE SYSTEM RUNNING SMOOTHLY--LIKE A WELL-OILED MEDIKIDZ JET!

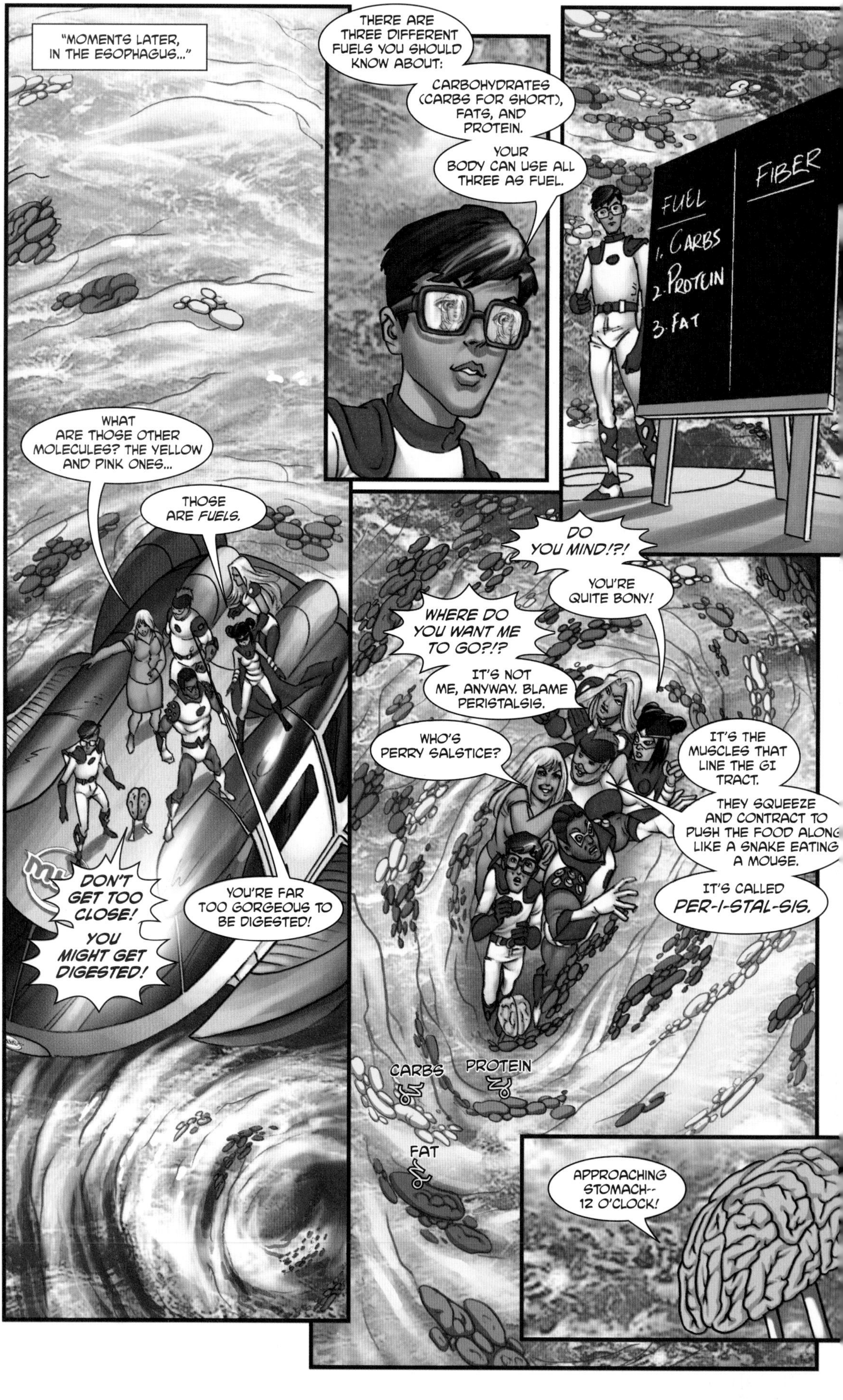
"MOMENTS LATER, IN THE ESOPHAGUS..."
THERE ARE THREE DIFFERENT FUELS YOU SHOULD KNOW ABOUT:
CARBOHYDRATES (CARBS FOR SHORT), FATS, AND PROTEIN.
YOUR BODY CAN USE ALL THREE AS FUEL.
FUEL
1. CARBS
2. PROTEIN
3. FAT
FIBER
WHAT ARE THOSE OTHER MOLECULES? THE YELLOW AND PINK ONES...
THOSE ARE *FUELS.*
DON'T GET TOO CLOSE! YOU MIGHT GET DIGESTED!
YOU'RE FAR TOO GORGEOUS TO BE DIGESTED!
DO YOU MIND!?!
YOU'RE QUITE BONY!
WHERE DO YOU WANT ME TO GO?!?
IT'S NOT ME, ANYWAY. BLAME PERISTALSIS.
WHO'S PERRY SALSTICE?
IT'S THE MUSCLES THAT LINE THE GI TRACT.
THEY SQUEEZE AND CONTRACT TO PUSH THE FOOD ALONG LIKE A SNAKE EATING A MOUSE.
IT'S CALLED *PER-I-STAL-SIS.*
CARBS
PROTEIN
FAT
APPROACHING STOMACH-- 12 O'CLOCK!

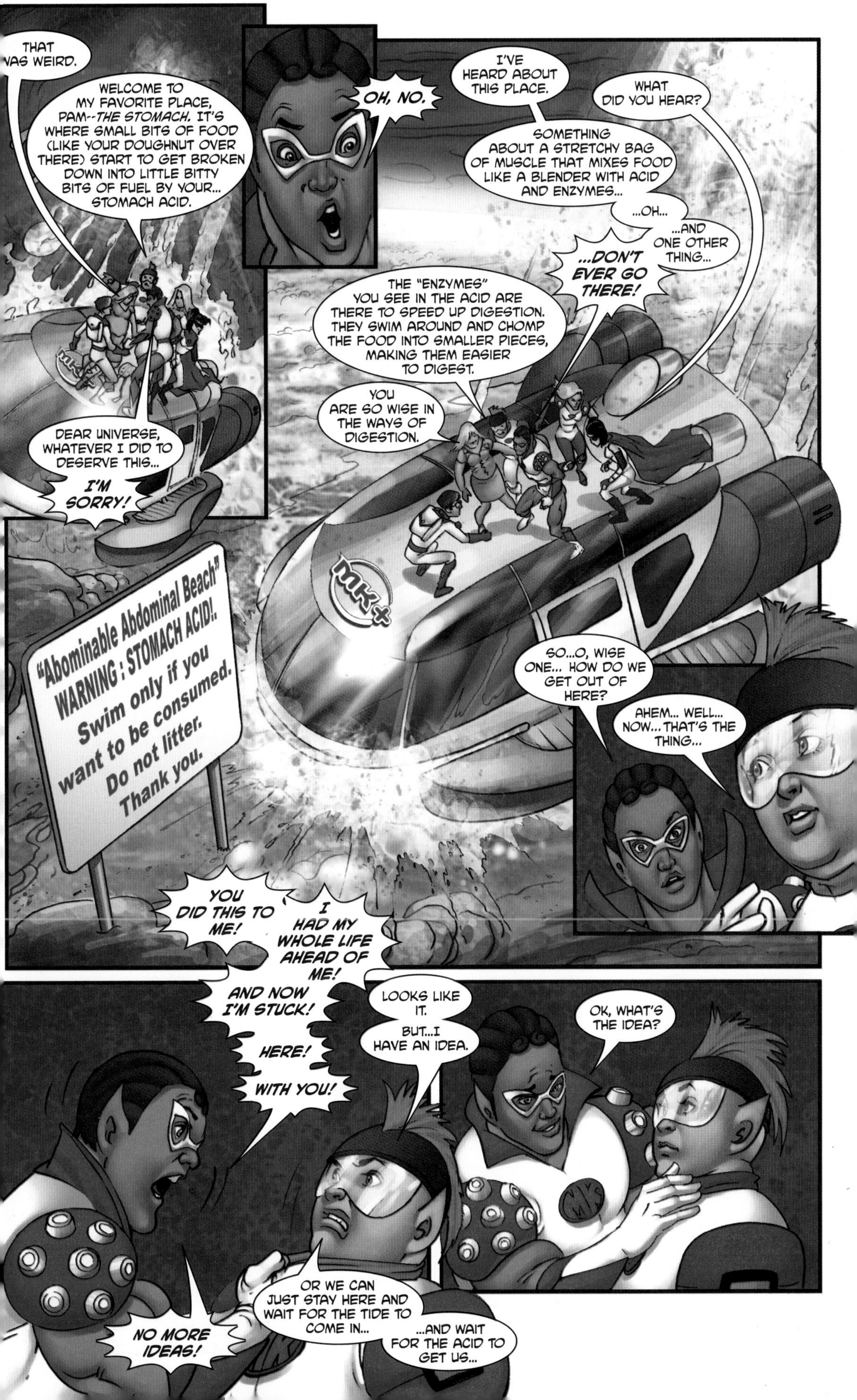
THAT WAS WEIRD.
WELCOME TO MY FAVORITE PLACE, PAM--*THE STOMACH.* IT'S WHERE SMALL BITS OF FOOD (LIKE YOUR DOUGHNUT OVER THERE) START TO GET BROKEN DOWN INTO LITTLE BITTY BITS OF FUEL BY YOUR... STOMACH ACID.
DEAR UNIVERSE, WHATEVER I DID TO DESERVE THIS...
I'M SORRY!
OH, NO.
I'VE HEARD ABOUT THIS PLACE.
WHAT DID YOU HEAR?
SOMETHING ABOUT A STRETCHY BAG OF MUSCLE THAT MIXES FOOD LIKE A BLENDER WITH ACID AND ENZYMES...
...OH...
...AND ONE OTHER THING...
...DON'T EVER GO THERE!
THE "ENZYMES" YOU SEE IN THE ACID ARE THERE TO SPEED UP DIGESTION. THEY SWIM AROUND AND CHOMP THE FOOD INTO SMALLER PIECES, MAKING THEM EASIER TO DIGEST.
YOU ARE SO WISE IN THE WAYS OF DIGESTION.
"Abominable Abdominal Beach"
WARNING : STOMACH ACID!.
Swim only if you want to be consumed.
Do not litter.
Thank you.
SO...O, WISE ONE... HOW DO WE GET OUT OF HERE?
AHEM... WELL... NOW...THAT'S THE THING...
YOU DID THIS TO ME!
I HAD MY WHOLE LIFE AHEAD OF ME!
AND NOW I'M STUCK!
HERE!
WITH YOU!
NO MORE IDEAS!
OR WE CAN JUST STAY HERE AND WAIT FOR THE TIDE TO COME IN...
...AND WAIT FOR THE ACID TO GET US...
LOOKS LIKE IT.
BUT...I HAVE AN IDEA.
OK, WHAT'S THE IDEA?

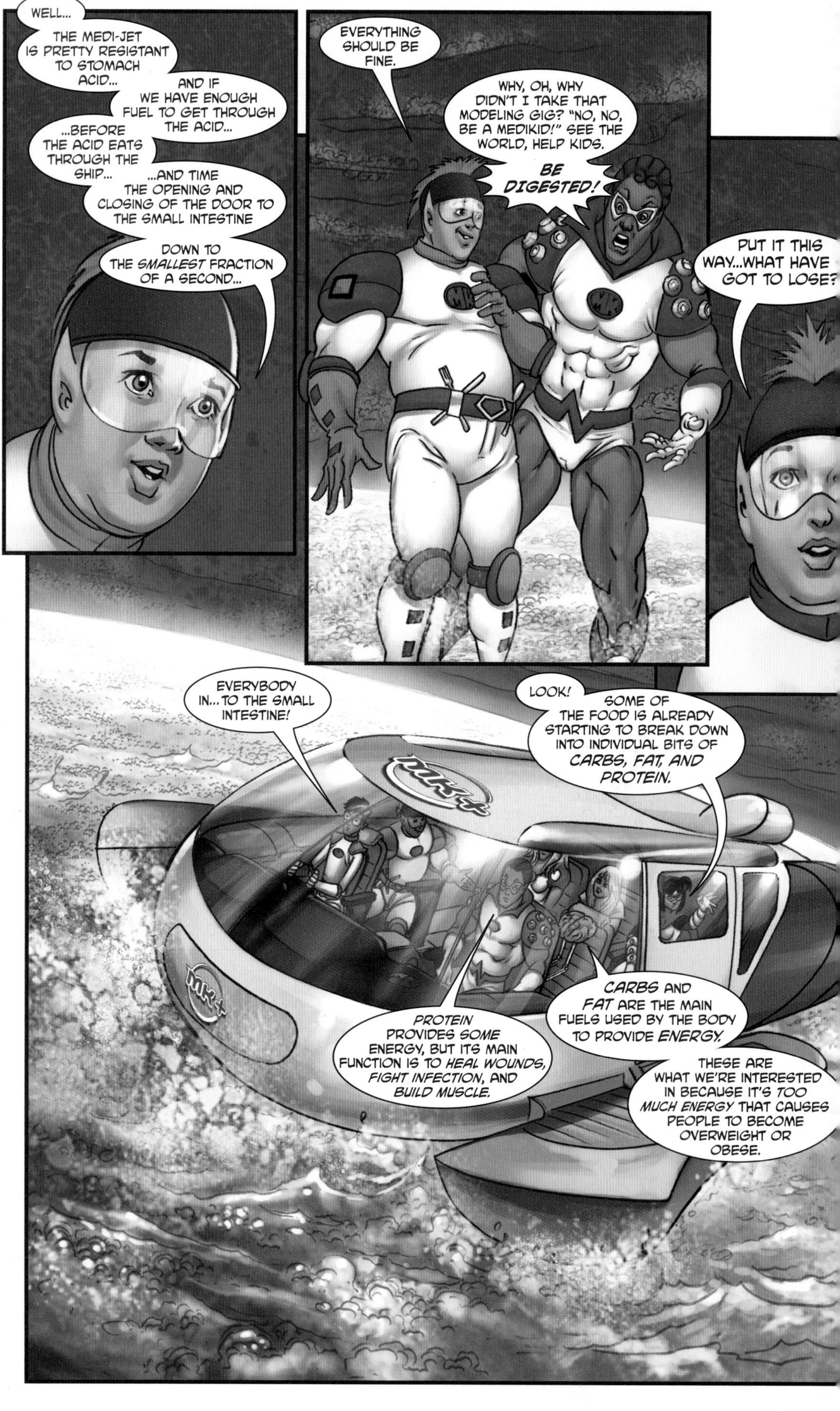
WELL...
THE MEDI-JET IS PRETTY RESISTANT TO STOMACH ACID...
AND IF WE HAVE ENOUGH FUEL TO GET THROUGH THE ACID...
...BEFORE THE ACID EATS THROUGH THE SHIP...
...AND TIME THE OPENING AND CLOSING OF THE DOOR TO THE SMALL INTESTINE
DOWN TO THE SMALLEST FRACTION OF A SECOND...
EVERYTHING SHOULD BE FINE.
WHY, OH, WHY DIDN'T I TAKE THAT MODELING GIG? "NO, NO, BE A MEDIKID!" SEE THE WORLD, HELP KIDS.
BE DIGESTED!
PUT IT THIS WAY...WHAT HAVE GOT TO LOSE?
EVERYBODY IN...TO THE SMALL INTESTINE!
LOOK!
SOME OF THE FOOD IS ALREADY STARTING TO BREAK DOWN INTO INDIVIDUAL BITS OF CARBS, FAT, AND PROTEIN.
CARBS AND FAT ARE THE MAIN FUELS USED BY THE BODY TO PROVIDE ENERGY.
PROTEIN PROVIDES SOME ENERGY, BUT ITS MAIN FUNCTION IS TO HEAL WOUNDS, FIGHT INFECTION, AND BUILD MUSCLE.
THESE ARE WHAT WE'RE INTERESTED IN BECAUSE IT'S TOO MUCH ENERGY THAT CAUSES PEOPLE TO BECOME OVERWEIGHT OR OBESE.

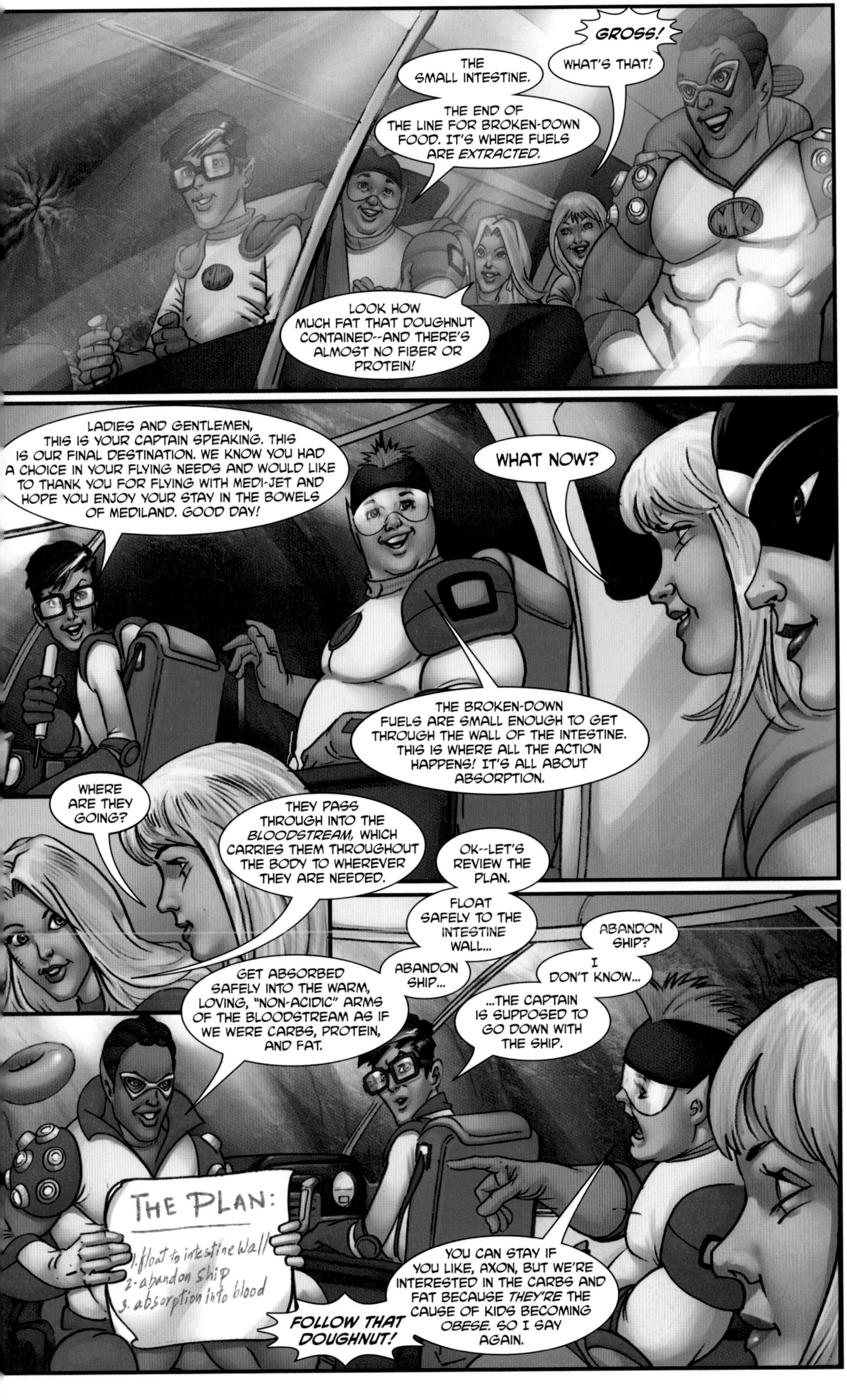
THE SMALL INTESTINE.
THE END OF THE LINE FOR BROKEN-DOWN FOOD. IT'S WHERE FUELS ARE EXTRACTED.
GROSS!
WHAT'S THAT!
LOOK HOW MUCH FAT THAT DOUGHNUT CONTAINED--AND THERE'S ALMOST NO FIBER OR PROTEIN!
LADIES AND GENTLEMEN, THIS IS YOUR CAPTAIN SPEAKING. THIS IS OUR FINAL DESTINATION. WE KNOW YOU HAD A CHOICE IN YOUR FLYING NEEDS AND WOULD LIKE TO THANK YOU FOR FLYING WITH MEDI-JET AND HOPE YOU ENJOY YOUR STAY IN THE BOWELS OF MEDILAND. GOOD DAY!
WHAT NOW?
THE BROKEN-DOWN FUELS ARE SMALL ENOUGH TO GET THROUGH THE WALL OF THE INTESTINE. THIS IS WHERE ALL THE ACTION HAPPENS! IT'S ALL ABOUT ABSORPTION.
WHERE ARE THEY GOING?
THEY PASS THROUGH INTO THE BLOODSTREAM, WHICH CARRIES THEM THROUGHOUT THE BODY TO WHEREVER THEY ARE NEEDED.
OK--LET'S REVIEW THE PLAN.
FLOAT SAFELY TO THE INTESTINE WALL...
ABANDON SHIP...
GET ABSORBED SAFELY INTO THE WARM, LOVING, "NON-ACIDIC" ARMS OF THE BLOODSTREAM AS IF WE WERE CARBS, PROTEIN, AND FAT.
ABANDON SHIP?
I DON'T KNOW...
...THE CAPTAIN IS SUPPOSED TO GO DOWN WITH THE SHIP.
THE PLAN:
1. float to intestine wall
2. abandon ship
3. absorption into blood
YOU CAN STAY IF YOU LIKE, AXON, BUT WE'RE INTERESTED IN THE CARBS AND FAT BECAUSE THEY'RE THE CAUSE OF KIDS BECOMING OBESE. SO I SAY AGAIN.
FOLLOW THAT DOUGHNUT!

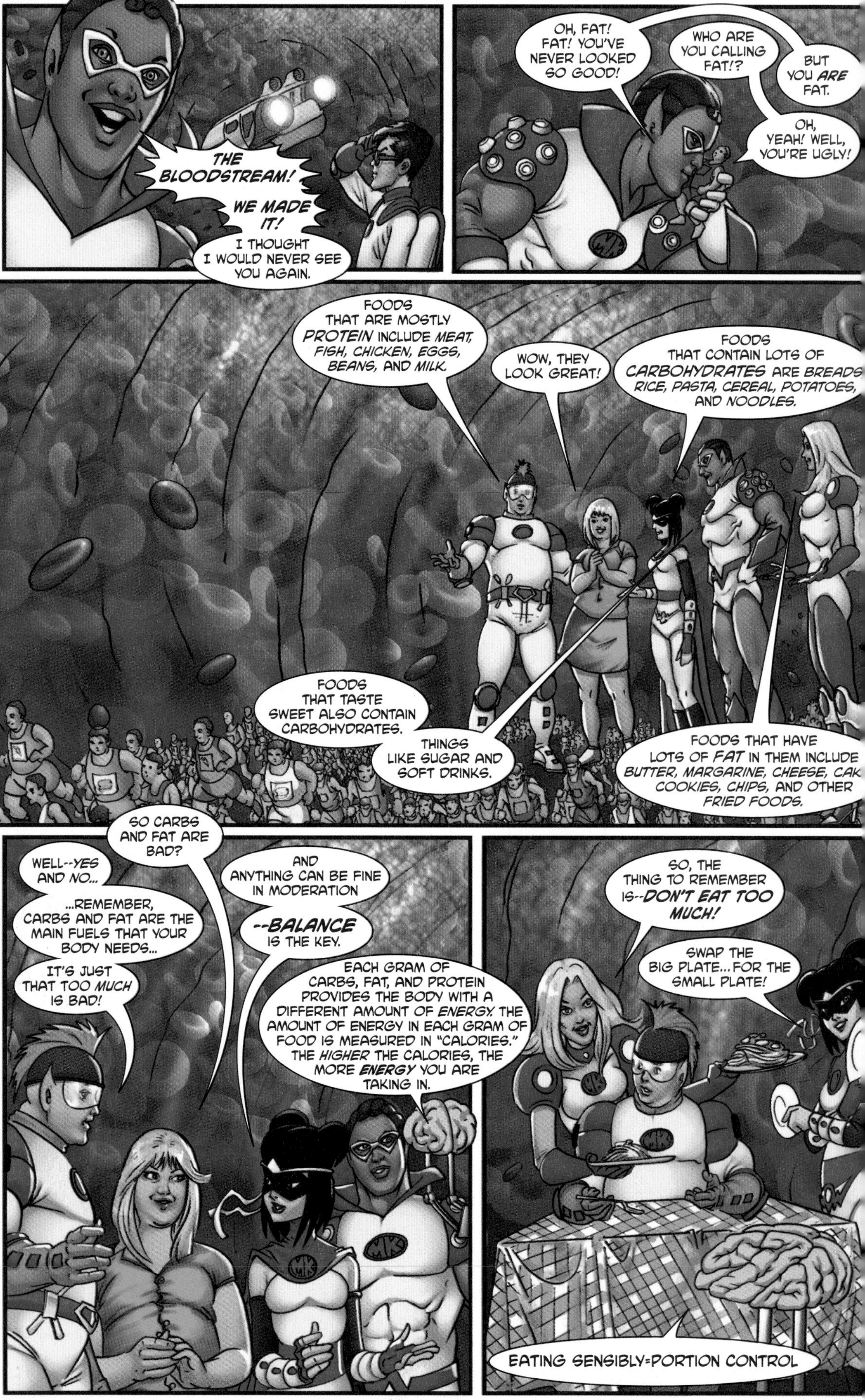
THE BLOODSTREAM!
WE MADE IT!
I THOUGHT I WOULD NEVER SEE YOU AGAIN.
OH, FAT! FAT! YOU'VE NEVER LOOKED SO GOOD!
WHO ARE YOU CALLING FAT!?
BUT YOU ARE FAT.
OH, YEAH! WELL, YOU'RE UGLY!
FOODS THAT ARE MOSTLY PROTEIN INCLUDE MEAT, FISH, CHICKEN, EGGS, BEANS, AND MILK.
WOW, THEY LOOK GREAT!
FOODS THAT CONTAIN LOTS OF CARBOHYDRATES ARE BREADS RICE, PASTA, CEREAL, POTATOES, AND NOODLES.
FOODS THAT TASTE SWEET ALSO CONTAIN CARBOHYDRATES.
THINGS LIKE SUGAR AND SOFT DRINKS.
FOODS THAT HAVE LOTS OF FAT IN THEM INCLUDE BUTTER, MARGARINE, CHEESE, CAK COOKIES, CHIPS, AND OTHER FRIED FOODS.
SO CARBS AND FAT ARE BAD?
WELL--YES AND NO...
...REMEMBER, CARBS AND FAT ARE THE MAIN FUELS THAT YOUR BODY NEEDS...
IT'S JUST THAT TOO MUCH IS BAD!
AND ANYTHING CAN BE FINE IN MODERATION
--BALANCE IS THE KEY.
EACH GRAM OF CARBS, FAT, AND PROTEIN PROVIDES THE BODY WITH A DIFFERENT AMOUNT OF ENERGY. THE AMOUNT OF ENERGY IN EACH GRAM OF FOOD IS MEASURED IN "CALORIES." THE HIGHER THE CALORIES, THE MORE ENERGY YOU ARE TAKING IN.
SO, THE THING TO REMEMBER IS--DON'T EAT TOO MUCH!
SWAP THE BIG PLATE...FOR THE SMALL PLATE!
EATING SENSIBLY=PORTION CONTROL

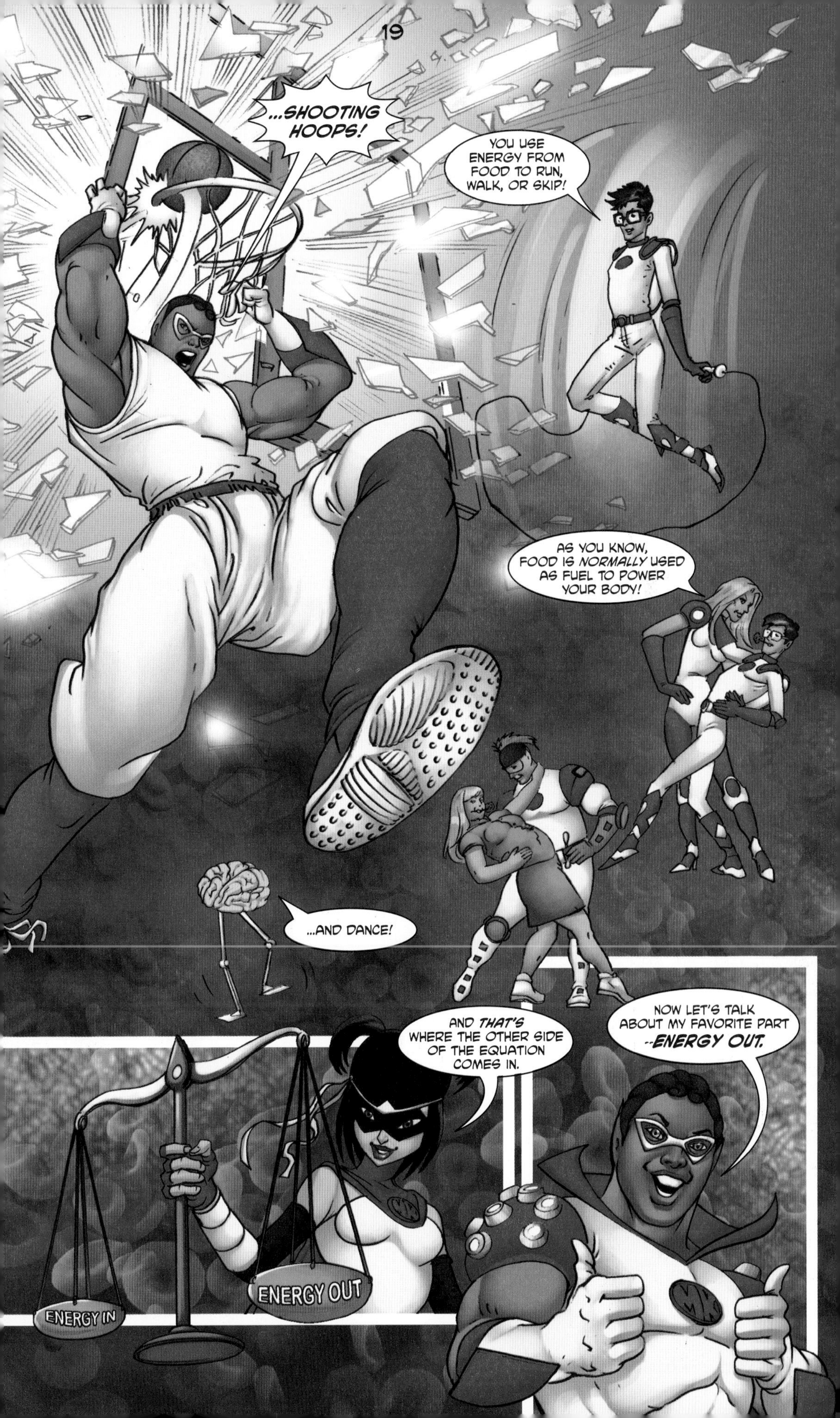
...SHOOTING HOOPS!
YOU USE ENERGY FROM FOOD TO RUN, WALK, OR SKIP!
AS YOU KNOW, FOOD IS NORMALLY USED AS FUEL TO POWER YOUR BODY!
...AND DANCE!
AND THAT'S WHERE THE OTHER SIDE OF THE EQUATION COMES IN.
NOW LET'S TALK ABOUT MY FAVORITE PART --ENERGY OUT.
ENERGY IN
ENERGY OUT

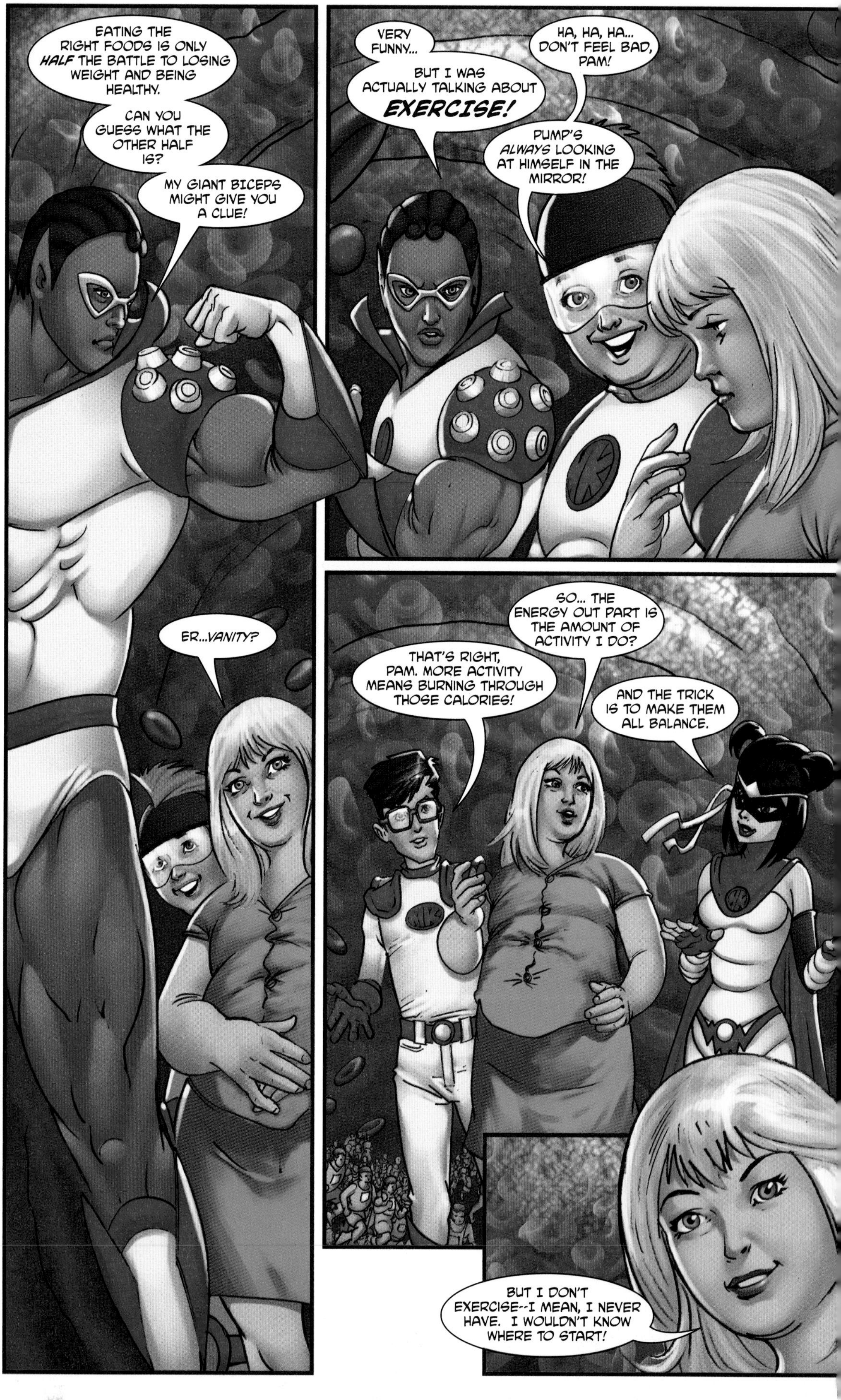
EATING THE RIGHT FOODS IS ONLY *HALF* THE BATTLE TO LOSING WEIGHT AND BEING HEALTHY.
CAN YOU GUESS WHAT THE OTHER HALF IS?
MY GIANT BICEPS MIGHT GIVE YOU A CLUE!
ER...*VANITY?*
VERY FUNNY...
BUT I WAS ACTUALLY TALKING ABOUT **EXERCISE!**
HA, HA, HA... DON'T FEEL BAD, PAM!
PUMP'S *ALWAYS* LOOKING AT HIMSELF IN THE MIRROR!
SO... THE ENERGY OUT PART IS THE AMOUNT OF ACTIVITY I DO?
THAT'S RIGHT, PAM. MORE ACTIVITY MEANS BURNING THROUGH THOSE CALORIES!
AND THE TRICK IS TO MAKE THEM ALL BALANCE.
BUT I DON'T EXERCISE--I MEAN, I NEVER HAVE. I WOULDN'T KNOW WHERE TO START!

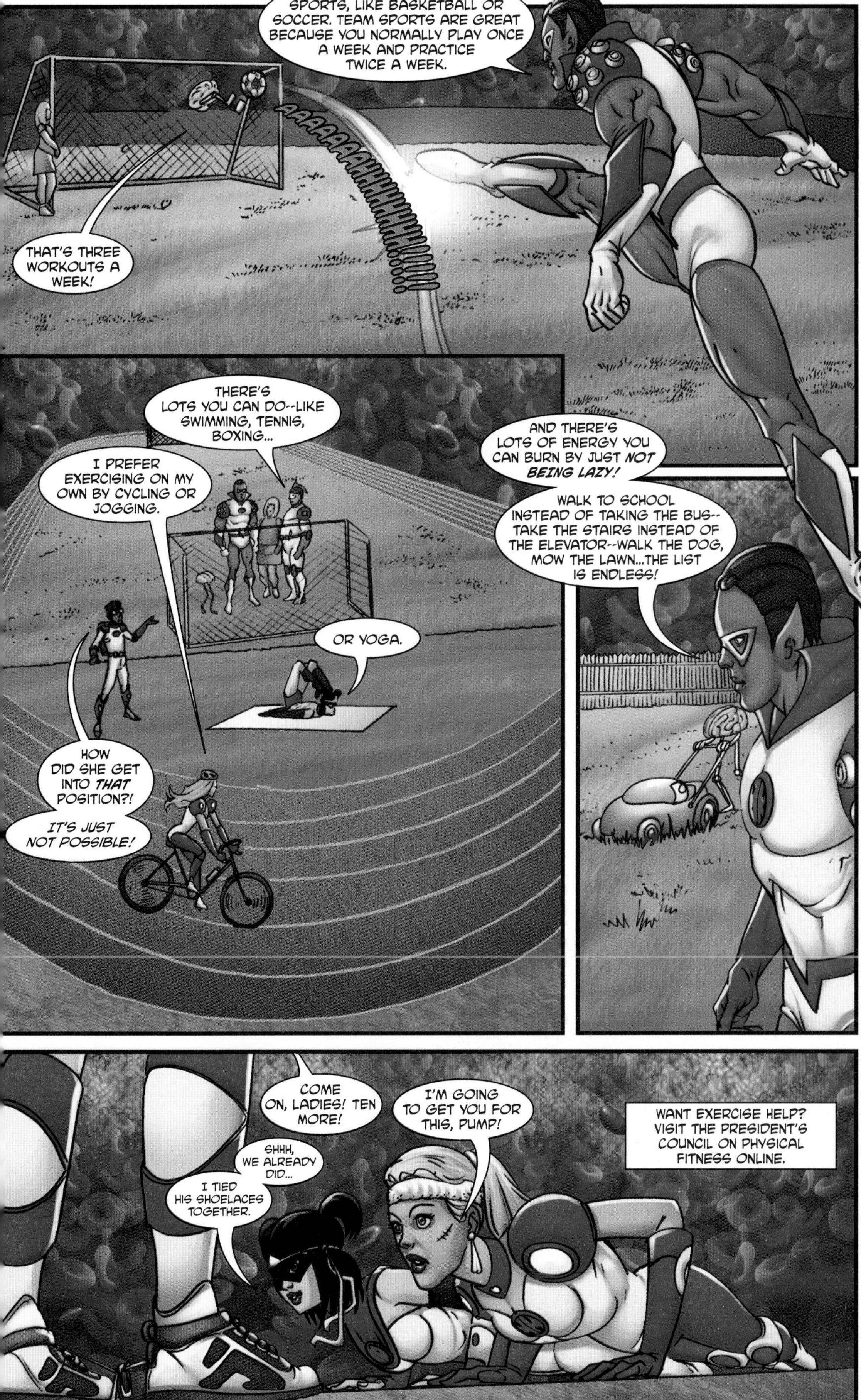
GET INVOLVED IN TEAM SPORTS, LIKE BASKETBALL OR SOCCER. TEAM SPORTS ARE GREAT BECAUSE YOU NORMALLY PLAY ONCE A WEEK AND PRACTICE TWICE A WEEK.
AAAAAAAHHHHHHHHH!!!!!!
THAT'S THREE WORKOUTS A WEEK!
THERE'S LOTS YOU CAN DO--LIKE SWIMMING, TENNIS, BOXING...
I PREFER EXERCISING ON MY OWN BY CYCLING OR JOGGING.
OR YOGA.
HOW DID SHE GET INTO *THAT* POSITION?!
IT'S JUST NOT POSSIBLE!
AND THERE'S LOTS OF ENERGY YOU CAN BURN BY JUST *NOT BEING LAZY!*
WALK TO SCHOOL INSTEAD OF TAKING THE BUS--TAKE THE STAIRS INSTEAD OF THE ELEVATOR--WALK THE DOG, MOW THE LAWN...THE LIST IS ENDLESS!
COME ON, LADIES! TEN MORE!
I'M GOING TO GET YOU FOR THIS, PUMP!
SHHH, WE ALREADY DID...
I TIED HIS SHOELACES TOGETHER.
WANT EXERCISE HELP? VISIT THE PRESIDENT'S COUNCIL ON PHYSICAL FITNESS ONLINE.

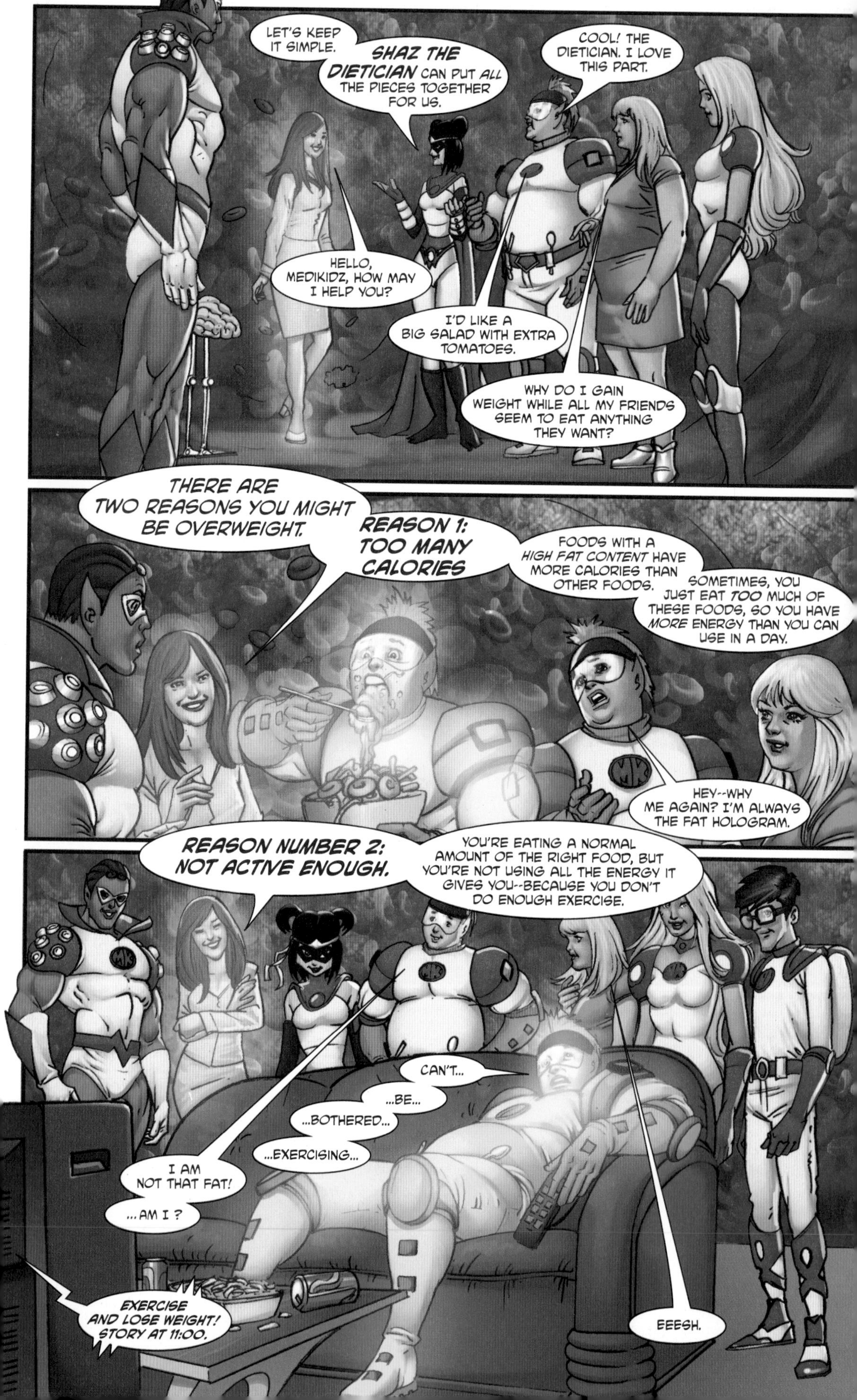
LET'S KEEP IT SIMPLE.
SHAZ THE DIETICIAN CAN PUT ALL THE PIECES TOGETHER FOR US.
COOL! THE DIETICIAN. I LOVE THIS PART.
HELLO, MEDIKIDZ, HOW MAY I HELP YOU?
I'D LIKE A BIG SALAD WITH EXTRA TOMATOES.
WHY DO I GAIN WEIGHT WHILE ALL MY FRIENDS SEEM TO EAT ANYTHING THEY WANT?
THERE ARE TWO REASONS YOU MIGHT BE OVERWEIGHT.
REASON 1: TOO MANY CALORIES
FOODS WITH A HIGH FAT CONTENT HAVE MORE CALORIES THAN OTHER FOODS.
SOMETIMES, YOU JUST EAT TOO MUCH OF THESE FOODS, SO YOU HAVE MORE ENERGY THAN YOU CAN USE IN A DAY.
HEY--WHY ME AGAIN? I'M ALWAYS THE FAT HOLOGRAM.
REASON NUMBER 2: NOT ACTIVE ENOUGH.
YOU'RE EATING A NORMAL AMOUNT OF THE RIGHT FOOD, BUT YOU'RE NOT USING ALL THE ENERGY IT GIVES YOU--BECAUSE YOU DON'T DO ENOUGH EXERCISE.
CAN'T...
...BE...
...BOTHERED...
...EXERCISING...
I AM NOT THAT FAT!
...AM I ?
EXERCISE AND LOSE WEIGHT! STORY AT 11:00.
EEESH.

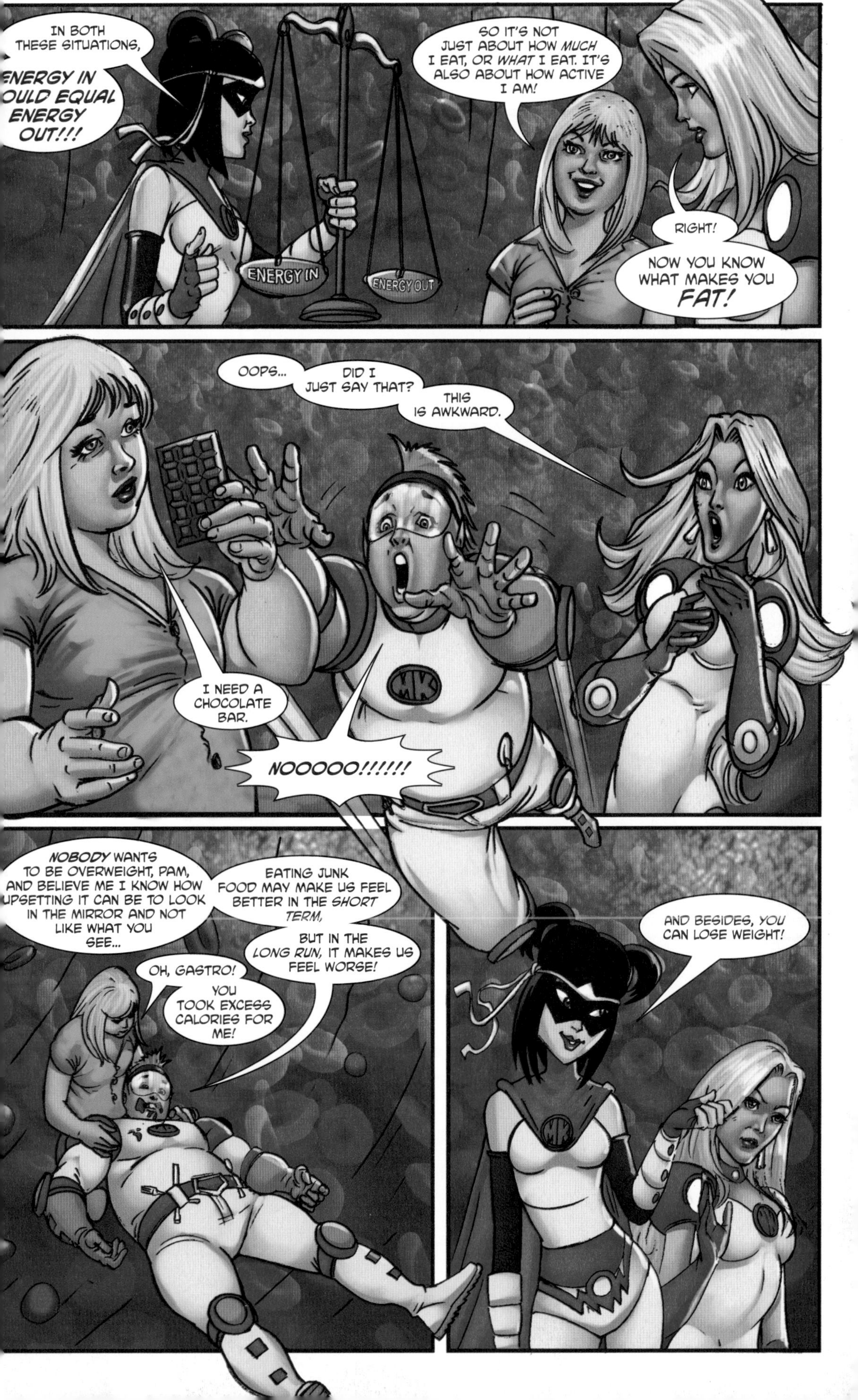
IN BOTH THESE SITUATIONS,
ENERGY IN OULD EQUAL ENERGY OUT!!!
ENERGY IN
ENERGY OUT
SO IT'S NOT JUST ABOUT HOW MUCH I EAT, OR WHAT I EAT. IT'S ALSO ABOUT HOW ACTIVE I AM!
RIGHT!
NOW YOU KNOW WHAT MAKES YOU FAT!
OOPS...
DID I JUST SAY THAT?
THIS IS AWKWARD.
I NEED A CHOCOLATE BAR.
NOOOOO!!!!!!
MK
NOBODY WANTS TO BE OVERWEIGHT, PAM, AND BELIEVE ME I KNOW HOW UPSETTING IT CAN BE TO LOOK IN THE MIRROR AND NOT LIKE WHAT YOU SEE...
EATING JUNK FOOD MAY MAKE US FEEL BETTER IN THE SHORT TERM,
BUT IN THE LONG RUN, IT MAKES US FEEL WORSE!
OH, GASTRO!
YOU TOOK EXCESS CALORIES FOR ME!
AND BESIDES, YOU CAN LOSE WEIGHT!

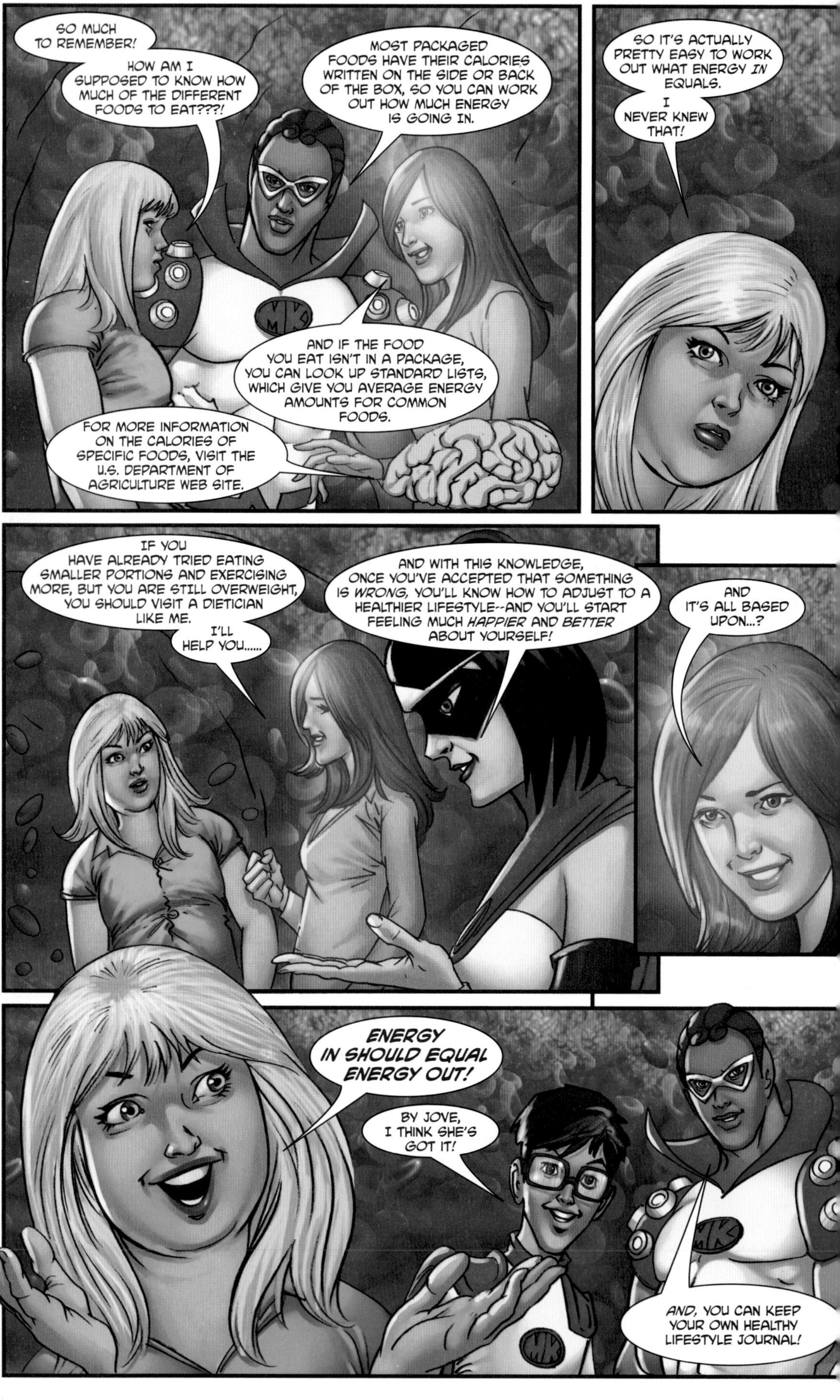
SO MUCH TO REMEMBER!
HOW AM I SUPPOSED TO KNOW HOW MUCH OF THE DIFFERENT FOODS TO EAT???!
MOST PACKAGED FOODS HAVE THEIR CALORIES WRITTEN ON THE SIDE OR BACK OF THE BOX, SO YOU CAN WORK OUT HOW MUCH ENERGY IS GOING IN.
AND IF THE FOOD YOU EAT ISN'T IN A PACKAGE, YOU CAN LOOK UP STANDARD LISTS, WHICH GIVE YOU AVERAGE ENERGY AMOUNTS FOR COMMON FOODS.
FOR MORE INFORMATION ON THE CALORIES OF SPECIFIC FOODS, VISIT THE U.S. DEPARTMENT OF AGRICULTURE WEB SITE.
SO IT'S ACTUALLY PRETTY EASY TO WORK OUT WHAT ENERGY *IN* EQUALS.
I NEVER KNEW THAT!
IF YOU HAVE ALREADY TRIED EATING SMALLER PORTIONS AND EXERCISING MORE, BUT YOU ARE STILL OVERWEIGHT, YOU SHOULD VISIT A DIETICIAN LIKE ME.
I'LL HELP YOU......
AND WITH THIS KNOWLEDGE, ONCE YOU'VE ACCEPTED THAT SOMETHING IS *WRONG,* YOU'LL KNOW HOW TO ADJUST TO A HEALTHIER LIFESTYLE--AND YOU'LL START FEELING MUCH *HAPPIER* AND *BETTER* ABOUT YOURSELF!
AND IT'S ALL BASED UPON...?
ENERGY IN SHOULD EQUAL ENERGY OUT!
BY JOVE, I THINK SHE'S GOT IT!
AND, YOU CAN KEEP YOUR OWN HEALTHY LIFESTYLE JOURNAL!

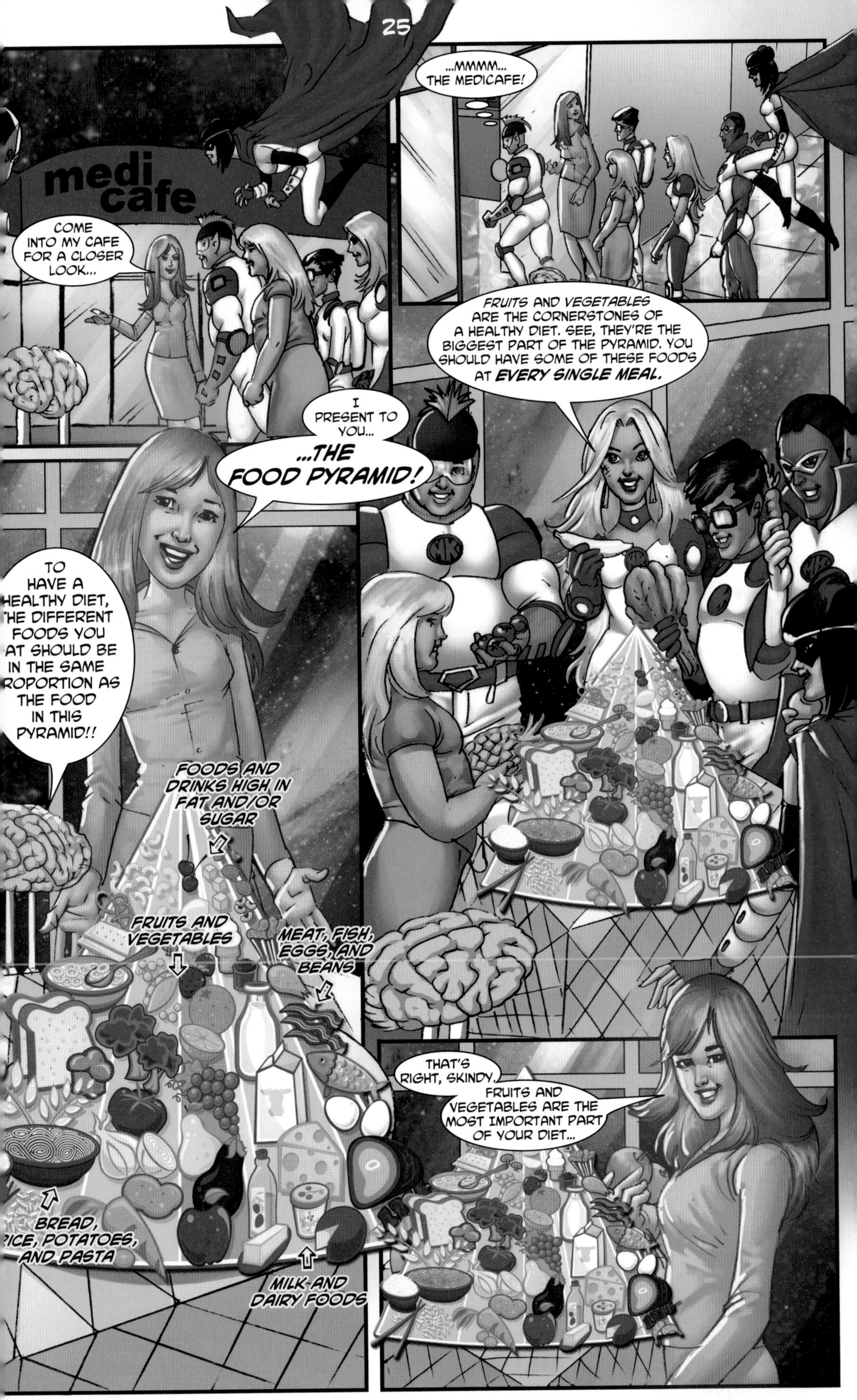
medi cafe
COME INTO MY CAFE FOR A CLOSER LOOK...
...MMMM... THE MEDICAFE!
I PRESENT TO YOU...
...THE FOOD PYRAMID!
TO HAVE A HEALTHY DIET, THE DIFFERENT FOODS YOU AT SHOULD BE IN THE SAME ROPORTION AS THE FOOD IN THIS PYRAMID!!
FOODS AND DRINKS HIGH IN FAT AND/OR SUGAR
FRUITS AND VEGETABLES
MEAT, FISH, EGGS, AND BEANS
BREAD, RICE, POTATOES, AND PASTA
MILK AND DAIRY FOODS
FRUITS AND VEGETABLES ARE THE CORNERSTONES OF A HEALTHY DIET. SEE, THEY'RE THE BIGGEST PART OF THE PYRAMID. YOU SHOULD HAVE SOME OF THESE FOODS AT EVERY SINGLE MEAL.
THAT'S RIGHT, SKINDY.
FRUITS AND VEGETABLES ARE THE MOST IMPORTANT PART OF YOUR DIET...

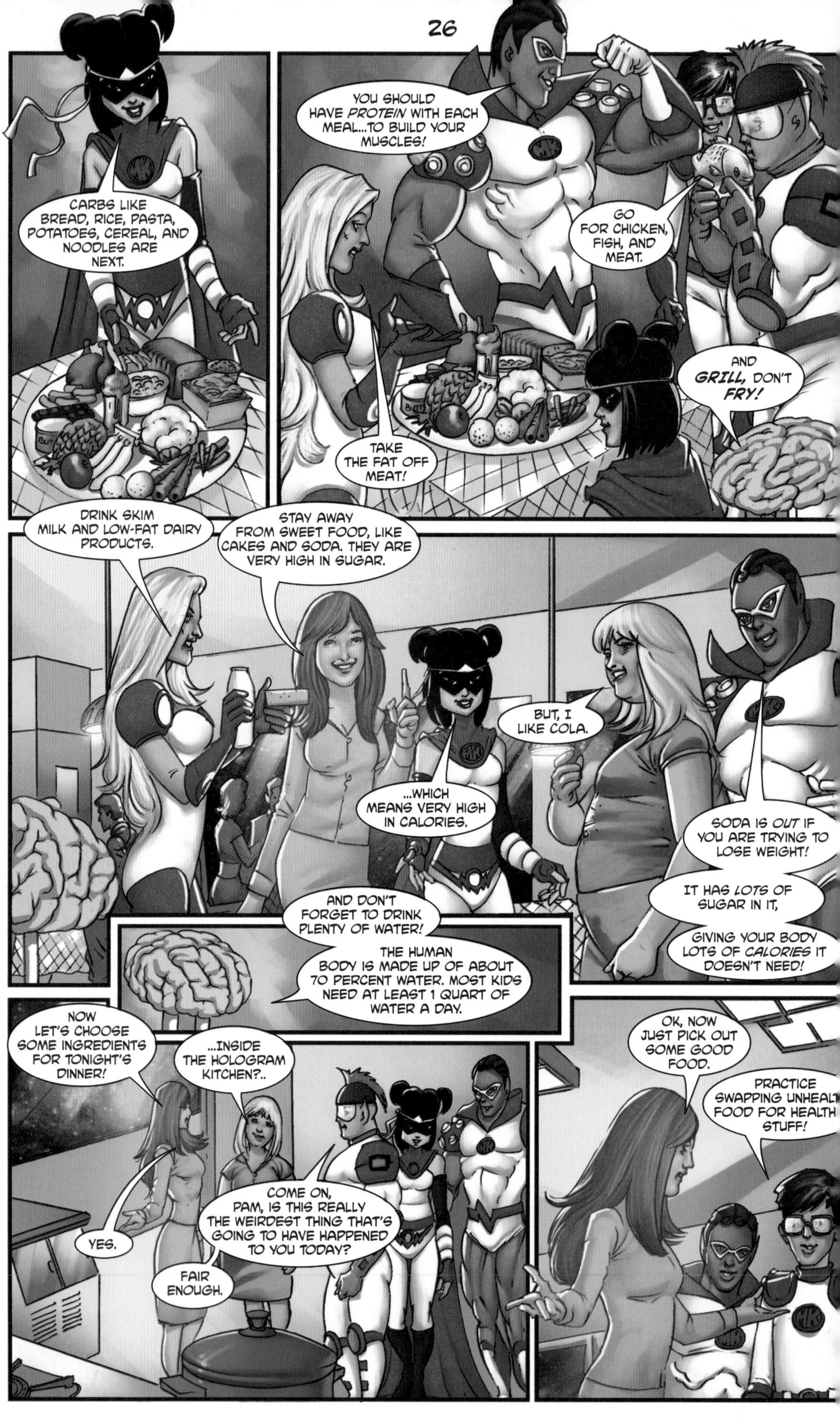
CARBS LIKE BREAD, RICE, PASTA, POTATOES, CEREAL, AND NOODLES ARE NEXT.
YOU SHOULD HAVE *PROTEIN* WITH EACH MEAL...TO BUILD YOUR MUSCLES!
GO FOR CHICKEN, FISH, AND MEAT.
TAKE THE FAT OFF MEAT!
AND **GRILL,** DON'T ***FRY!***
DRINK SKIM MILK AND LOW-FAT DAIRY PRODUCTS.
STAY AWAY FROM SWEET FOOD, LIKE CAKES AND SODA. THEY ARE VERY HIGH IN SUGAR.
...WHICH MEANS VERY HIGH IN CALORIES.
BUT, I LIKE COLA.
SODA IS *OUT* IF YOU ARE TRYING TO LOSE WEIGHT!
IT HAS *LOTS OF* SUGAR IN IT,
GIVING YOUR BODY LOTS OF *CALORIES* IT DOESN'T NEED!
AND DON'T FORGET TO DRINK PLENTY OF WATER!
THE HUMAN BODY IS MADE UP OF ABOUT 70 PERCENT WATER. MOST KIDS NEED AT LEAST 1 QUART OF WATER A DAY.
NOW LET'S CHOOSE SOME INGREDIENTS FOR TONIGHT'S DINNER!
...INSIDE THE HOLOGRAM KITCHEN?..
YES.
COME ON, PAM, IS THIS REALLY THE WEIRDEST THING THAT'S GOING TO HAVE HAPPENED TO YOU TODAY?
FAIR ENOUGH.
OK, NOW JUST PICK OUT SOME GOOD FOOD.
PRACTICE SWAPPING UNHEAL FOOD FOR HEALTH STUFF!

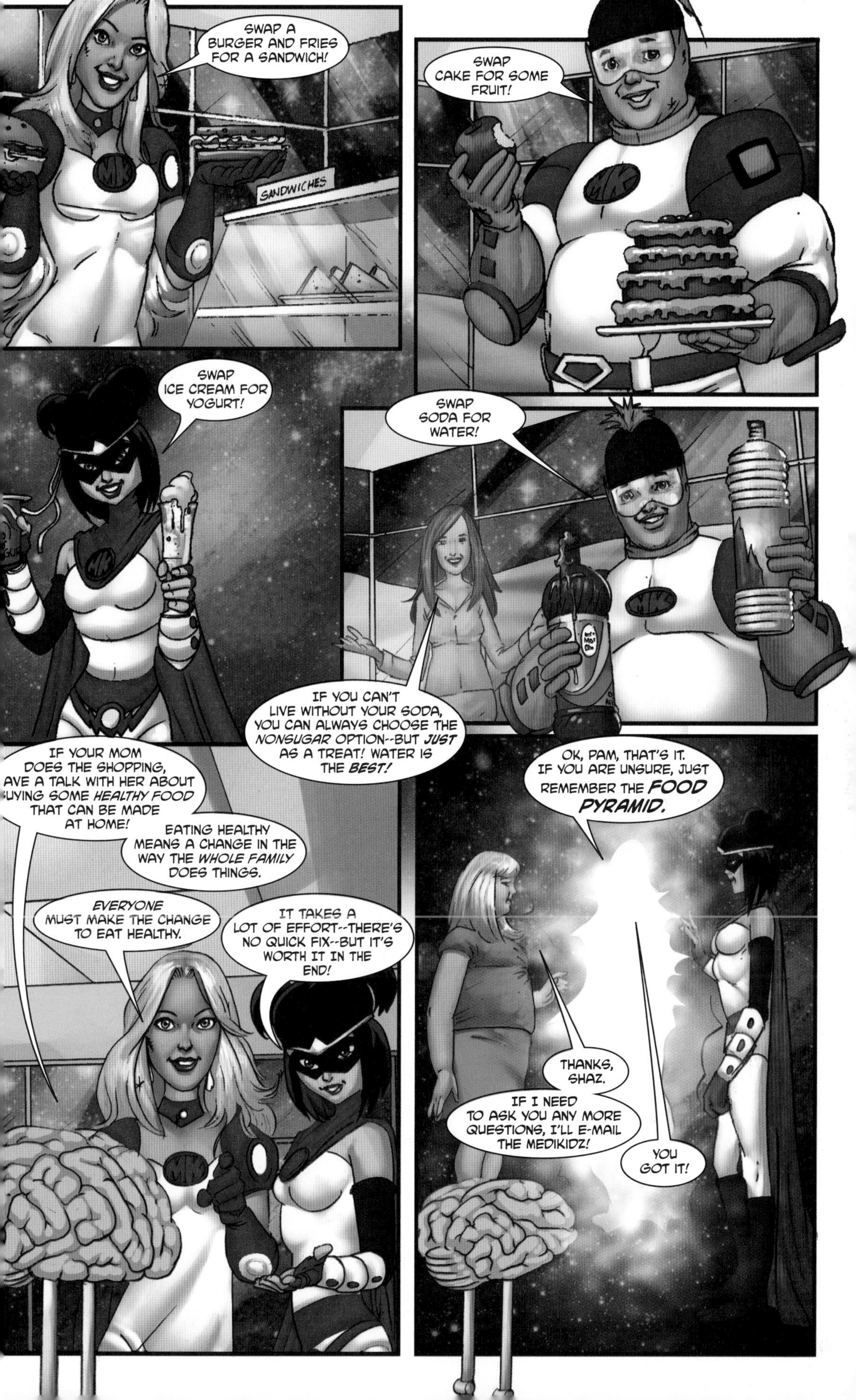
SWAP A BURGER AND FRIES FOR A SANDWICH!
SANDWICHES
SWAP CAKE FOR SOME FRUIT!
SWAP ICE CREAM FOR YOGURT!
SWAP SODA FOR WATER!
IF YOU CAN'T LIVE WITHOUT YOUR SODA, YOU CAN ALWAYS CHOOSE THE *NONSUGAR* OPTION--BUT *JUST* AS A TREAT! WATER IS THE *BEST!*
IF YOUR MOM DOES THE SHOPPING, AVE A TALK WITH HER ABOUT UYING SOME *HEALTHY FOOD* THAT CAN BE MADE AT HOME!
EATING HEALTHY MEANS A CHANGE IN THE WAY THE *WHOLE FAMILY* DOES THINGS.
EVERYONE MUST MAKE THE CHANGE TO EAT HEALTHY.
IT TAKES A LOT OF EFFORT--THERE'S NO QUICK FIX--BUT IT'S WORTH IT IN THE END!
OK, PAM, THAT'S IT. IF YOU ARE UNSURE, JUST REMEMBER THE ***FOOD PYRAMID.***
THANKS, SHAZ.
IF I NEED TO ASK YOU ANY MORE QUESTIONS, I'LL E-MAIL THE MEDIKIDZ!
YOU GOT IT!

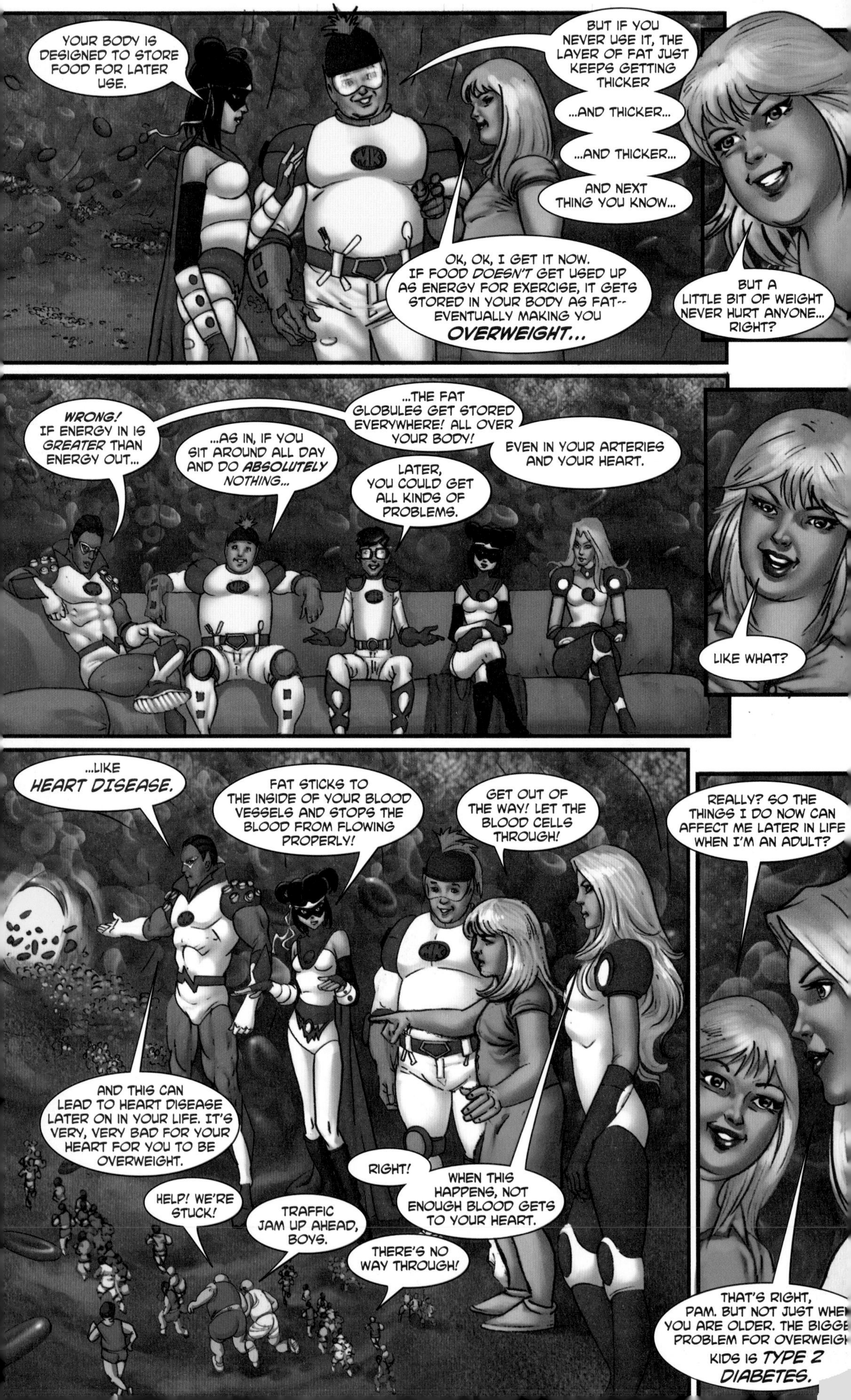
YOUR BODY IS DESIGNED TO STORE FOOD FOR LATER USE.
BUT IF YOU NEVER USE IT, THE LAYER OF FAT JUST KEEPS GETTING THICKER
...AND THICKER...
...AND THICKER...
AND NEXT THING YOU KNOW...
OK, OK, I GET IT NOW. IF FOOD *DOESN'T* GET USED UP AS ENERGY FOR EXERCISE, IT GETS STORED IN YOUR BODY AS FAT-- EVENTUALLY MAKING YOU **OVERWEIGHT...**
BUT A LITTLE BIT OF WEIGHT NEVER HURT ANYONE... RIGHT?
WRONG! IF ENERGY IN IS *GREATER* THAN ENERGY OUT...
...AS IN, IF YOU SIT AROUND ALL DAY AND DO ***ABSOLUTELY*** *NOTHING...*
...THE FAT GLOBULES GET STORED EVERYWHERE! ALL OVER YOUR BODY!
EVEN IN YOUR ARTERIES AND YOUR HEART.
LATER, YOU COULD GET ALL KINDS OF PROBLEMS.
LIKE WHAT?
...LIKE ***HEART DISEASE.***
FAT STICKS TO THE INSIDE OF YOUR BLOOD VESSELS AND STOPS THE BLOOD FROM FLOWING PROPERLY!
GET OUT OF THE WAY! LET THE BLOOD CELLS THROUGH!
REALLY? SO THE THINGS I DO NOW CAN AFFECT ME LATER IN LIFE WHEN I'M AN ADULT?
AND THIS CAN LEAD TO HEART DISEASE LATER ON IN YOUR LIFE. IT'S VERY, VERY BAD FOR YOUR HEART FOR YOU TO BE OVERWEIGHT.
RIGHT!
WHEN THIS HAPPENS, NOT ENOUGH BLOOD GETS TO YOUR HEART.
HELP! WE'RE STUCK!
TRAFFIC JAM UP AHEAD, BOYS.
THERE'S NO WAY THROUGH!
THAT'S RIGHT, PAM. BUT NOT JUST WHE YOU ARE OLDER. THE BIGGE PROBLEM FOR OVERWEIG KIDS IS ***TYPE 2 DIABETES.***

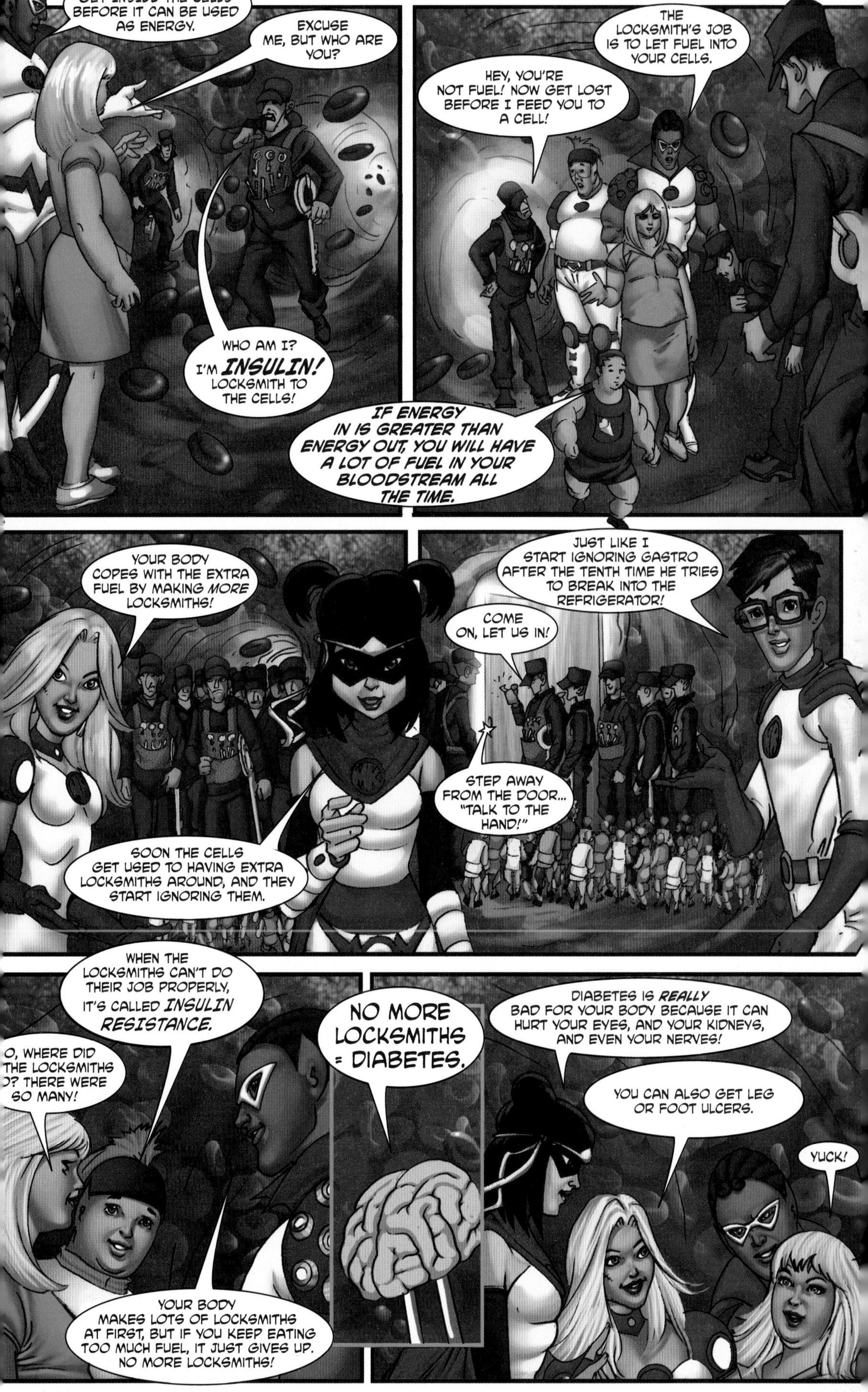
FUEL HAS TO GET INSIDE THE CELLS BEFORE IT CAN BE USED AS ENERGY.
EXCUSE ME, BUT WHO ARE YOU?
WHO AM I? I'M INSULIN! LOCKSMITH TO THE CELLS!
THE LOCKSMITH'S JOB IS TO LET FUEL INTO YOUR CELLS.
HEY, YOU'RE NOT FUEL! NOW GET LOST BEFORE I FEED YOU TO A CELL!
IF ENERGY IN IS GREATER THAN ENERGY OUT, YOU WILL HAVE A LOT OF FUEL IN YOUR BLOODSTREAM ALL THE TIME.
YOUR BODY COPES WITH THE EXTRA FUEL BY MAKING MORE LOCKSMITHS!
SOON THE CELLS GET USED TO HAVING EXTRA LOCKSMITHS AROUND, AND THEY START IGNORING THEM.
JUST LIKE I START IGNORING GASTRO AFTER THE TENTH TIME HE TRIES TO BREAK INTO THE REFRIGERATOR!
COME ON, LET US IN!
STEP AWAY FROM THE DOOR... "TALK TO THE HAND!"
O, WHERE DID THE LOCKSMITHS O? THERE WERE SO MANY!
WHEN THE LOCKSMITHS CAN'T DO THEIR JOB PROPERLY, IT'S CALLED INSULIN RESISTANCE.
YOUR BODY MAKES LOTS OF LOCKSMITHS AT FIRST, BUT IF YOU KEEP EATING TOO MUCH FUEL, IT JUST GIVES UP. NO MORE LOCKSMITHS!
NO MORE LOCKSMITHS = DIABETES.
DIABETES IS REALLY BAD FOR YOUR BODY BECAUSE IT CAN HURT YOUR EYES, AND YOUR KIDNEYS, AND EVEN YOUR NERVES!
YOU CAN ALSO GET LEG OR FOOT ULCERS.
YUCK!

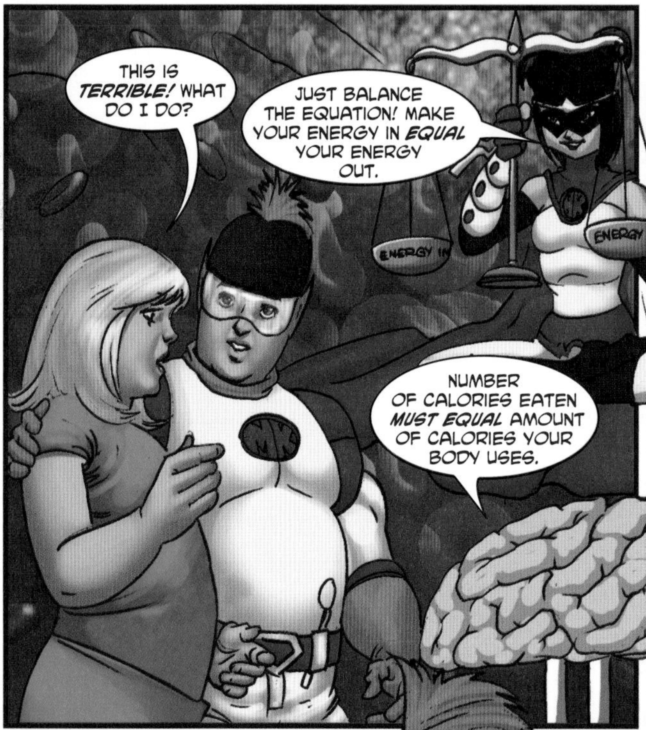
THIS IS *TERRIBLE!* WHAT DO I DO?
JUST BALANCE THE EQUATION! MAKE YOUR ENERGY IN *EQUAL* YOUR ENERGY OUT.
ENERGY IN
ENERGY OUT
NUMBER OF CALORIES EATEN *MUST EQUAL* AMOUNT OF CALORIES YOUR BODY USES.

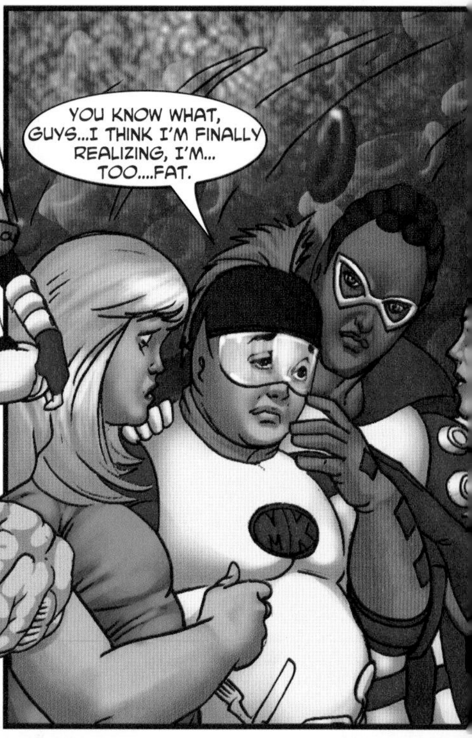
YOU KNOW WHAT, GUYS...I THINK I'M FINALLY REALIZING, I'M... TOO....FAT.

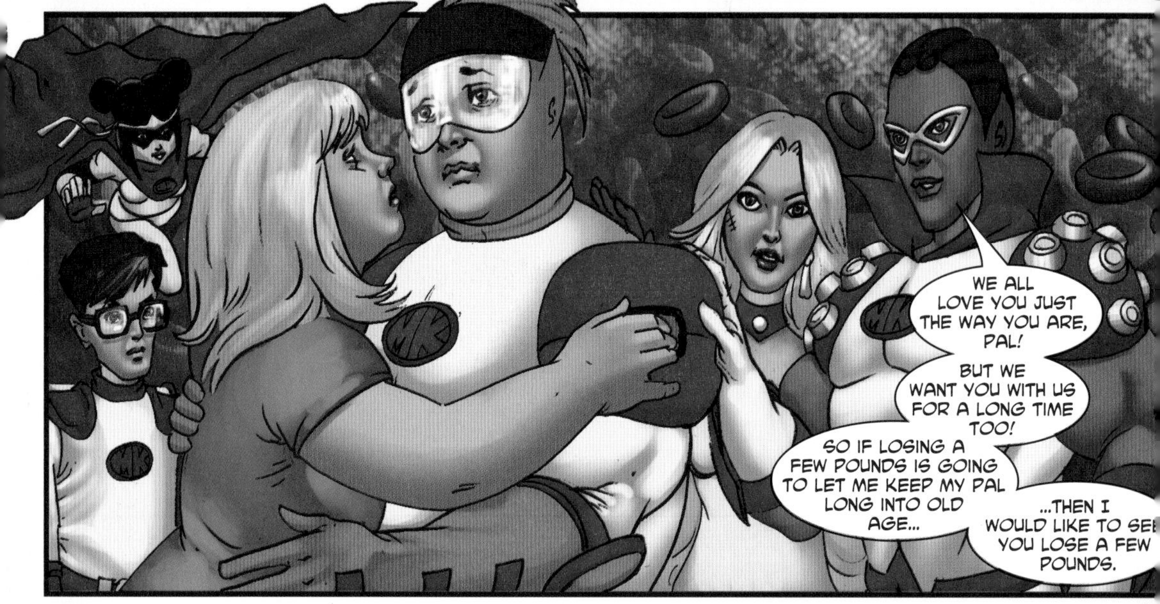
WE ALL LOVE YOU JUST THE WAY YOU ARE, PAL!
BUT WE WANT YOU WITH US FOR A LONG TIME TOO!
SO IF LOSING A FEW POUNDS IS GOING TO LET ME KEEP MY PAL LONG INTO OLD AGE...
...THEN I WOULD LIKE TO SEE YOU LOSE A FEW POUNDS.

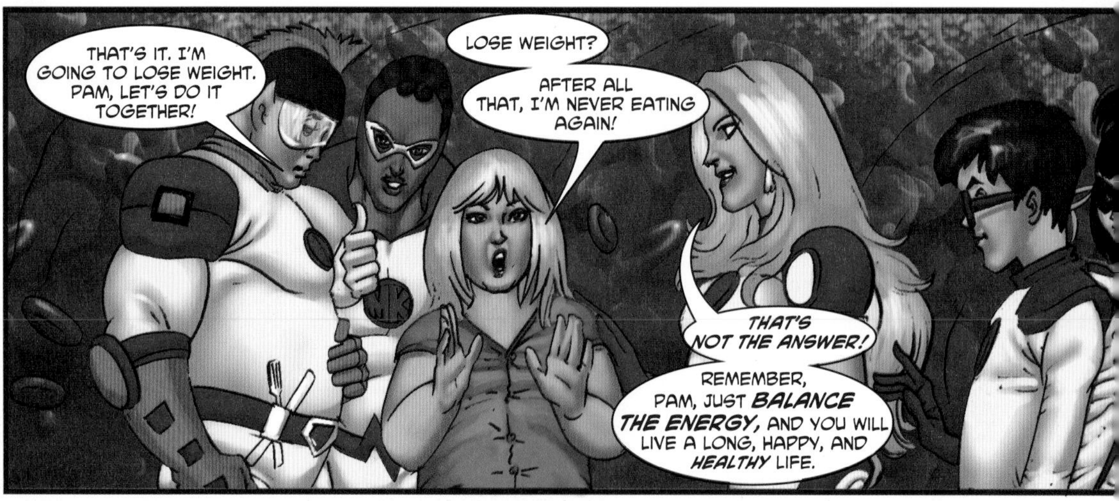
THAT'S IT. I'M GOING TO LOSE WEIGHT. PAM, LET'S DO IT TOGETHER!
LOSE WEIGHT?
AFTER ALL THAT, I'M NEVER EATING AGAIN!
THAT'S NOT THE ANSWER!
REMEMBER, PAM, JUST ***BALANCE THE ENERGY,*** AND YOU WILL LIVE A LONG, HAPPY, AND ***HEALTHY*** LIFE.

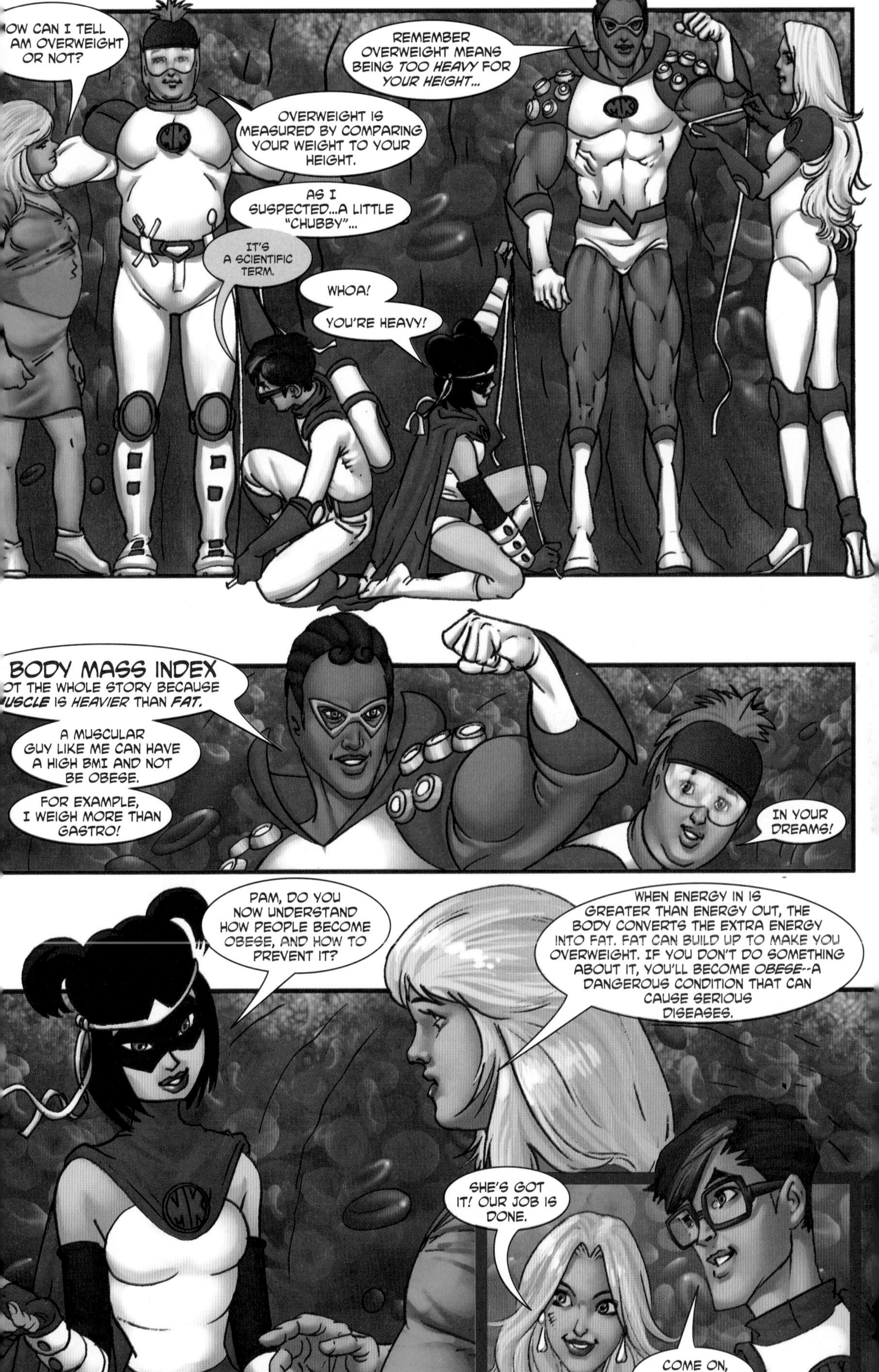
OW CAN I TELL
AM OVERWEIGHT
OR NOT?
OVERWEIGHT IS MEASURED BY COMPARING YOUR WEIGHT TO YOUR HEIGHT.
REMEMBER OVERWEIGHT MEANS BEING *TOO HEAVY* FOR *YOUR HEIGHT*...
AS I SUSPECTED...A LITTLE "CHUBBY"...
IT'S A SCIENTIFIC TERM.
WHOA!
YOU'RE HEAVY!
BODY MASS INDEX
OT THE WHOLE STORY BECAUSE
USCLE IS *HEAVIER* THAN *FAT*.
A MUSCULAR GUY LIKE ME CAN HAVE A HIGH BMI AND NOT BE OBESE.
FOR EXAMPLE, I WEIGH MORE THAN GASTRO!
IN YOUR DREAMS!
PAM, DO YOU NOW UNDERSTAND HOW PEOPLE BECOME OBESE, AND HOW TO PREVENT IT?
WHEN ENERGY IN IS GREATER THAN ENERGY OUT, THE BODY CONVERTS THE EXTRA ENERGY INTO FAT. FAT CAN BUILD UP TO MAKE YOU OVERWEIGHT. IF YOU DON'T DO SOMETHING ABOUT IT, YOU'LL BECOME *OBESE*--A DANGEROUS CONDITION THAT CAN CAUSE SERIOUS DISEASES.
SHE'S GOT IT! OUR JOB IS DONE.
COME ON, GUYS--TO THE MEDI-JET!

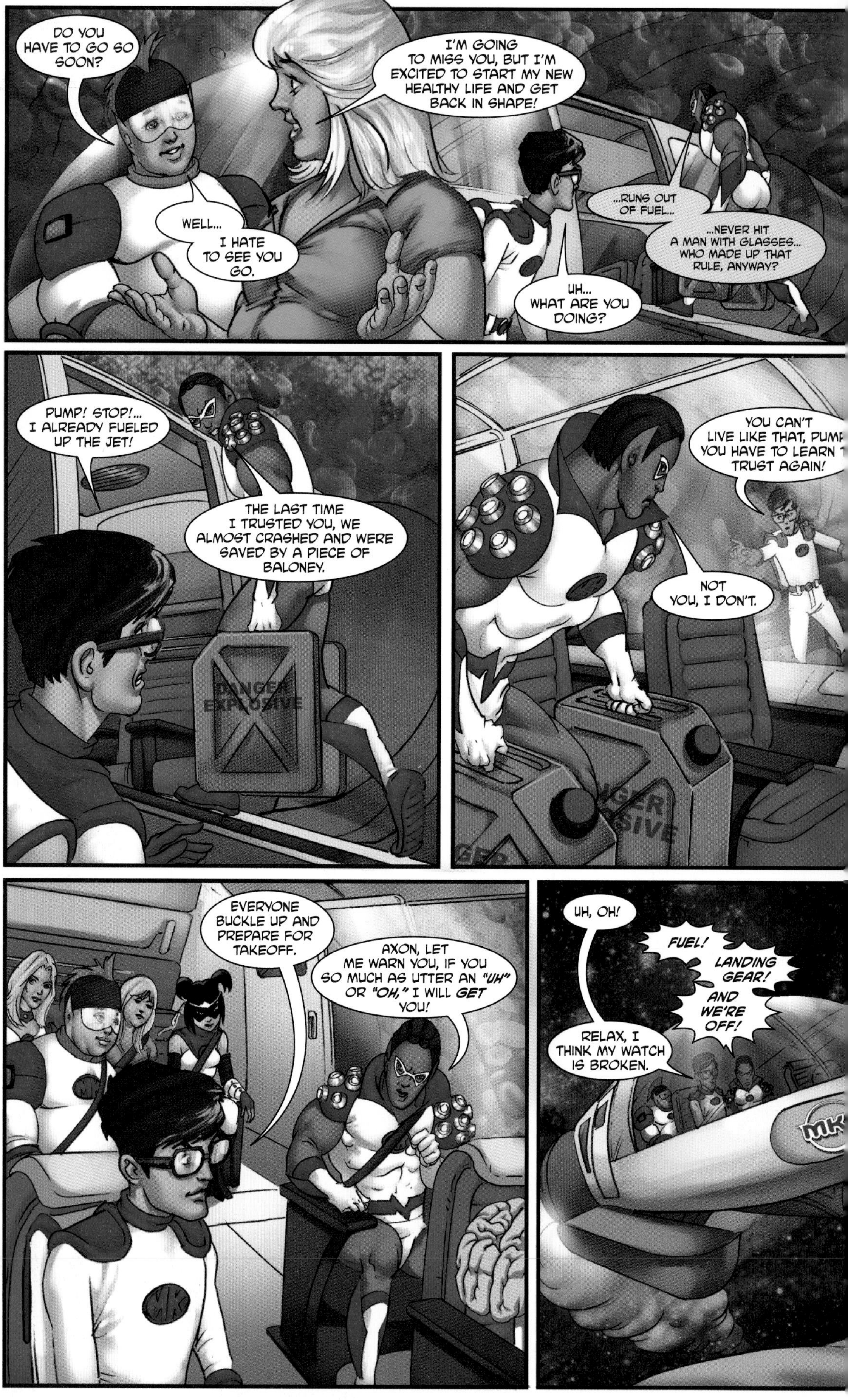
DO YOU HAVE TO GO SO SOON?
I'M GOING TO MISS YOU, BUT I'M EXCITED TO START MY NEW HEALTHY LIFE AND GET BACK IN SHAPE!
WELL... I HATE TO SEE YOU GO.
...RUNS OUT OF FUEL...
...NEVER HIT A MAN WITH GLASSES... WHO MADE UP THAT RULE, ANYWAY?
UH... WHAT ARE YOU DOING?
PUMP! STOP!... I ALREADY FUELED UP THE JET!
THE LAST TIME I TRUSTED YOU, WE ALMOST CRASHED AND WERE SAVED BY A PIECE OF BALONEY.
DANGER EXPLOSIVE
YOU CAN'T LIVE LIKE THAT, PUMP YOU HAVE TO LEARN TRUST AGAIN!
NOT YOU, I DON'T.
EVERYONE BUCKLE UP AND PREPARE FOR TAKEOFF.
AXON, LET ME WARN YOU, IF YOU SO MUCH AS UTTER AN "UH" OR "OH," I WILL GET YOU!
UH, OH!
FUEL!
LANDING GEAR!
AND WE'RE OFF!
RELAX, I THINK MY WATCH IS BROKEN.
MK

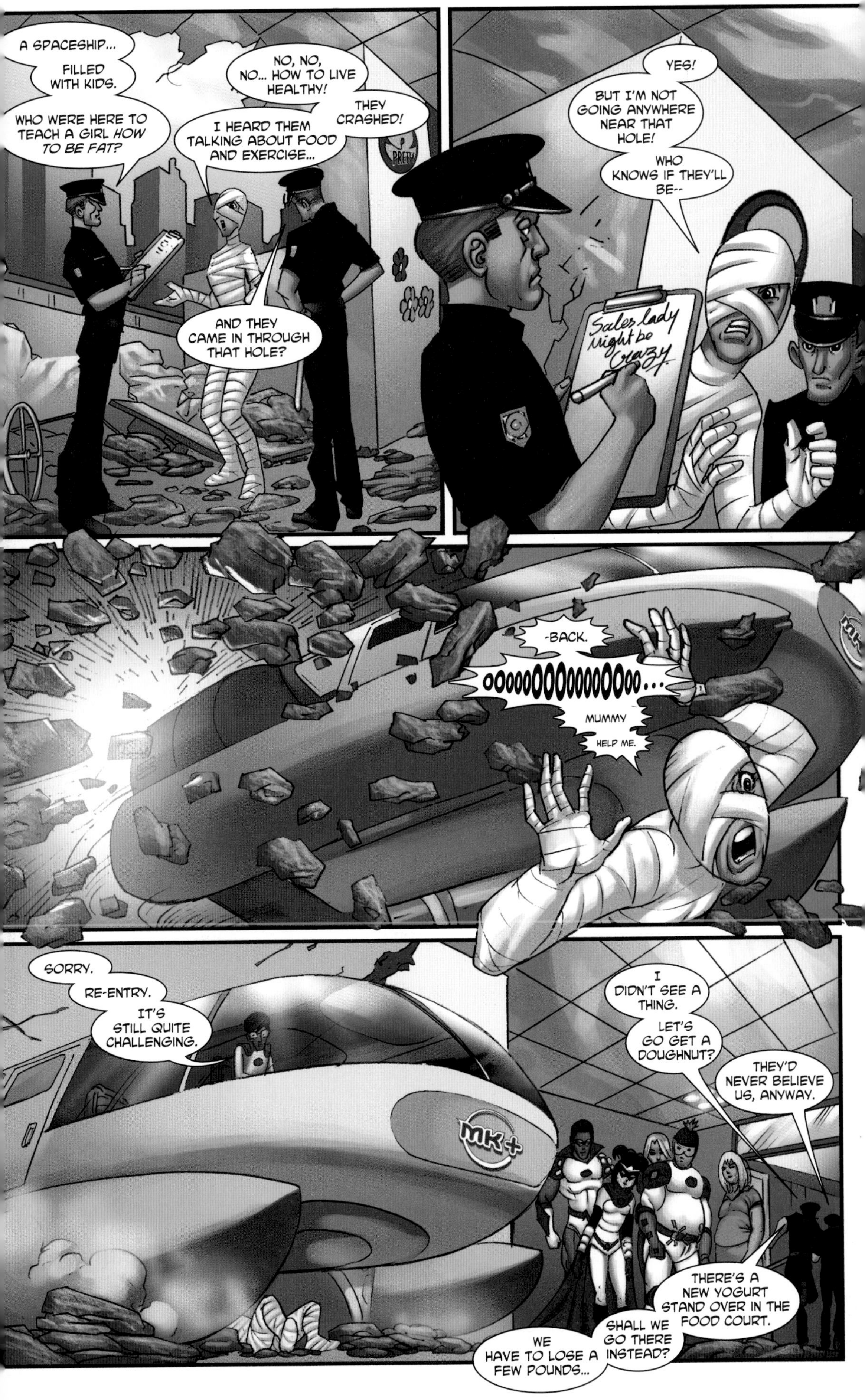
A SPACESHIP...
FILLED WITH KIDS.
WHO WERE HERE TO TEACH A GIRL *HOW* TO BE FAT?
NO, NO, NO... HOW TO LIVE HEALTHY!
THEY CRASHED!
I HEARD THEM TALKING ABOUT FOOD AND EXERCISE...
AND THEY CAME IN THROUGH THAT HOLE?
YES!
BUT I'M NOT GOING ANYWHERE NEAR THAT HOLE!
WHO KNOWS IF THEY'LL BE--
Sales lady might be crazy
-BACK.
OOOOOOOOOOOOOOOOO...
MUMMY
HELP ME.
SORRY.
RE-ENTRY.
IT'S STILL QUITE CHALLENGING.
I DIDN'T SEE A THING.
LET'S GO GET A DOUGHNUT?
THEY'D NEVER BELIEVE US, ANYWAY.
THERE'S A NEW YOGURT STAND OVER IN THE FOOD COURT.
SHALL WE GO THERE INSTEAD?
WE HAVE TO LOSE A FEW POUNDS...

SWAP ***UNHEALTHY*** FOODS FOR ***HEALTHIER*** ONES.

ALWAYS START THE DAY WITH A HEALTHY ***BREAKFAST,*** LIKE GRANOLA WITH YOGURT AND FRUIT. AIM TO HAVE ***VEGETABLES*** WITH YOUR LUNCH AND YOUR DINNER. EAT FRESH ***FRUIT*** EVERY DAY.

GET YOUR ***FAMILY*** TO EAT HEALTHY AND GET ACTIVE! IT'S EASIER AS A ***TEAM.***

DON'T TEASE OVERWEIGHT KIDS. IT CAN MAKE THEIR PROBLEM WORSE.

EXERCISE EVERY DAY. ***ANY*** EXERCISE IS GOOD, INCLUDING RIDING A BIKE, DANCING, SWIMMING, PLAYING SPORTS, AND SHOOTING HOOPS!

STOP EATING AS ***SOON*** AS YOU ARE SATISFIED--NOT WHEN YOU ARE SO FULL YOU COULDN'T EAT ANOTHER BITE!

HIGH-ENERGY FOODS LIKE CHOCOLATE, FRIES, CAKES, AND PIZZA ARE ***TREATS.*** YOU CAN STILL HAVE THEM, BUT SAVE THEM FOR SPECIAL OCCASIONS LIKE BIRTHDAYS!

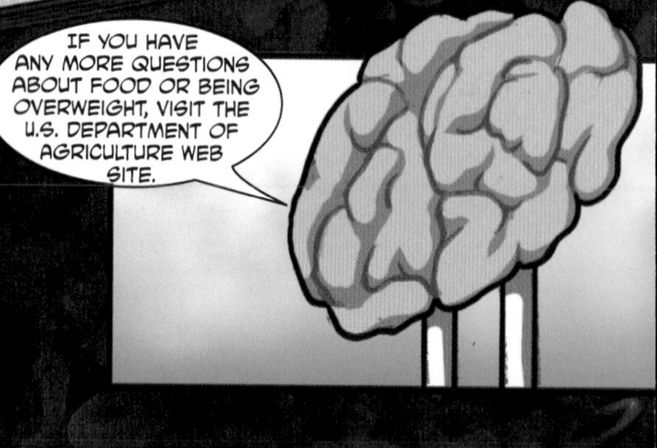
IF YOU HAVE ANY MORE QUESTIONS ABOUT FOOD OR BEING OVERWEIGHT, VISIT THE U.S. DEPARTMENT OF AGRICULTURE WEB SITE.

GLOSSARY

BODY MASS INDEX (BMI) A NUMBER CALCULATED FROM A
PERSON'S WEIGHT AND HEIGHT THAT MEASURES A PERSON'S
AMOUNT OF BODY FAT.

CALORIES A UNIT OF MEASUREMENT THAT REPRESENTS THE
AMOUNT OF ENERGY IN FOOD.

CARBOHYDRATES SUGAR MOLECULES OR CHAINS OF SUGAR
MOLECULES THAT ARE BROKEN DOWN BY THE BODY AND
USED AS THE MAJOR SOURCE OF ENERGY.

DIETICIAN TRAINED PROFESSIONALS WHO PLAN FOOD AND NUTRI-
TION PROGRAMS FOR INDIVIDUALS AND CAN OVERSEE MEAL
PREPARATION TO ENSURE THE HIGHEST LEVEL OF NUTRITION.

DIGESTION A PROCESS WHEREIN FOOD IS MIXED WITH DIGESTIVE
JUICES AS IT MOVES THROUGH THE DIGESTIVE TRACT AND IS
BROKEN DOWN INTO SMALLER MOLECULES, WHICH ARE
ABSORBED BY THE BODY, PROVIDING NECESSARY NUTRIENTS.

ENERGY AN ENTITY OF NATURE WHERE LEVELS OF FUEL MAKE IT
POSSIBLE FOR A BODY TO FUNCTION.

ENZYMES PROTEINS THAT SPEED UP CHEMICAL REACTIONS IN
THE BODY THAT RESULT IN THE BREAKDOWN OF MOLECULES.

ESOPHAGUS THE TUBE THAT CONNECTS THE THROAT WITH THE
STOMACH. WHEN A PERSON SWALLOWS, THE WALLS OF THE
ESOPHAGUS CONTRACT TO PUSH FOOD DOWN INTO THE
STOMACH.

EXERCISE A PHYSICAL ACTIVITY THAT USES ENERGY.

FATS ORGANIC COMPOUNDS THAT ARE MADE UP OF CARBON,
HYDROGEN, AND OXYGEN; ONE OF THE THREE NUTRIENTS THAT
SUPPLY ENERGY TO THE BODY.

FIBER AN INDIGESTIBLE SUBSTANCE FOUND IN PLANTS THAT AIDS
IN DIGESTION.

GI TRACT THE GASTROINTESTINAL TRACT; THE PATHWAY OF
TUBES AND ORGANS WITHIN THE BODY THAT FOOD PASSES
THROUGH DURING THE PROCESS OF DIGESTION.

INDIGESTIBLE LACKING THE ABILITY TO BE BROKEN DOWN BY
DIGESTION.

INSULIN A PROTEIN THAT IS ESSENTIAL FOR THE METABOLISM OF
CARBOHYDRATES AND REGULATION OF GLUCOSE LEVELS IN
THE BLOOD.

OBESITY A MEDICAL CONDITION IN WHICH EXCESS BODY FAT HAS
ACCUMULATED TO THE POINT WHERE IT CAN AFFECT HEALTH;
DETERMINED BY A BMI OF 30 OR ABOVE.

OVERWEIGHT HAVING EXTRA BODY WEIGHT.

PERISTALSIS A SERIES OF MUSCLE CONTRACTIONS IN THE DIGESTIVE
TRACT THAT MOVES FOOD THROUGH THE DIGESTIVE SYSTEM.

PROTEIN ORGANIC MOLECULES MADE UP OF AMINO ACIDS THAT

PROVIDE ENERGY IN THE BODY.

SMALL INTESTINE THE PART OF THE DIGESTIVE TRACT WHERE NUTRIENTS ARE ABSORBED BY THE BODY.

STOMACH THE ORGAN IN THE DIGESTIVE SYSTEM WHERE THE BULK OF DIGESTION OCCURS.

TYPE II DIABETES A DISORDER WHERE CELLS DEVELOP A RESISTANCE TO INSULIN, RESULTING IN THE PANCREAS LOSING THE ABILITY TO PRODUCE INSULIN.

FOR MORE INFORMATION

AMERICAN DIABETES ASSOCIATION
1701 NORTH BEAUREGARD STREET
ALEXANDRIA, VA 22311
(800) 342-2383
WEB SITE: HTTP://WWW.DIABETES.ORG
AN ASSOCIATION THAT FUNDS RESEARCH TO PREVENT, CURE, AND
    MANAGE DIABETES; PROVIDES SERVICES TO COMMUNITIES;
    PROVIDES INFORMATION ABOUT THE DISEASE; AND PROTECTS
    HUMAN RIGHTS.

NATIONAL AGRICULTURE LIBRARY
FOOD AND NUTRITION INFORMATION CENTER
10301 BALTIMORE AVENUE
BELTSVILLE, MD 20705
WEB SITE: HTTP://WWW.NUTRITION.GOV
GOVERNMENT FOOD AND NUTRITION LIBRARY STAFFED BY
    REGISTERED DIETICIANS.

NATIONAL LIBRARY OF MEDICINE
8600 ROCKVILLE PIKE
BETHESDA, MD 20894
(888) 346-3656
WEB SITE: HTTP://WWW.NLM.NIH.GOV
THE WORLD'S LARGEST MEDICAL LIBRARY.

THE OBESITY SOCIETY
8630 FENTON STREET, SUITE 814
SILVER SPRING, MD 20910
(301) 563-6595
WEB SITE: HTTP://WWW.OBESITY.ORG
A SCIENTIFIC SOCIETY DEDICATED TO THE STUDY OF
    OBESITY, ENCOURAGING RESEARCH ON ITS CAUSES
    AND TREATMENT.

PRESIDENT'S COUNCIL ON PHYSICAL FITNESS AND SPORTS
DEPARTMENT W
200 INDEPENDENCE AVENUE SW
ROOM 738-H
WASHINGTON, DC 20201
(202) 690-9000
WEB SITE: HTTP://WWW.FITNESS.GOV
ADVISORY COMMITTEE OF VOLUNTEER CITIZENS WHO ADVISE THE

PRESIDENT ABOUT PHYSICAL ACTIVITY, FITNESS, AND SPORTS IN AMERICA.

PUBLIC HEALTH AGENCY OF CANADA
130 COLONNADE ROAD
A.L. 6501H
OTTAWA, ONTARIO K1A 0K9
CANADA
WEB SITE: HTTP://WWW.PUBLICHEALTH.GC.CA
AN AGENCY DEDICATED TO PROTECT AND IMPROVE THE HEALTH OF CANADIANS.

UNITED STATES DEPARTMENT OF AGRICULTURE
1400 INDEPENDENCE AVENUE SW
WASHINGTON, DC 20250
WEB SITE: HTTP://WWW.USDA.GOV
THE FEDERAL DEPARTMENT RESPONSIBLE FOR DEVELOPING AND EXECUTING GOVERNMENT POLICY ON FARMING, AGRICULTURE, AND FOOD IN THE UNITED STATES.

WEB SITES

DUE TO THE CHANGING NATURE OF INTERNET LINKS, ROSEN PUBLISHING HAS DEVELOPED AN ONLINE LIST OF WEB SITES RELATED TO THE SUBJECT OF THIS BOOK. THIS SITE IS UPDATED REGULARLY. PLEASE USE THIS LINK TO ACCESS THE LIST:

HTTP://WWW.ROSENLINKS.COM/MED/OBES

FOR FURTHER READING

BERG, FRANCES M. *UNDERAGE & OVERWEIGHT: AMERICA'S CHILDHOOD OBESITY EPIDEMIC--WHAT EVERY FAMILY NEEDS TO KNOW.* NEW YORK, NY: HATHERLEIGH PRESS, 2003.

BIJLEVELD, MARJOLIJN. *FOOD AND YOU: A GUIDE TO HEALTHY HABITS FOR TEENS.* SANTA BARBARA, CA: GREENWOOD, 2008.

D'ELGIN, TERSHIA. *WHAT SHOULD I EAT?: A COMPLETE GUIDE TO THE NEW FOOD PYRAMID.* NEW YORK, NY: BALLANTINE, 2005.

EARLES, KATHY A. *SCALE BACK! WHY CHILDHOOD OBESITY IS NOT JUST ABOUT WEIGHT.* MUNSTER, IN: HILTON PUBLISHING, 2009.

FREEDMAN, JERI. *UNDERSTANDING OBESITY: THE MENTAL AND PHYSICAL EFFECTS OF OBESITY.* NEW YORK, NY: ROSEN PUBLISHING, 2008.

HASSINK, SANDRA G., ED. *A PARENT'S GUIDE TO CHILDHOOD OBESITY: A ROADMAP TO HEALTH.* ELK GROVE VILLAGE, IL: AMERICAN ACADEMY OF PEDIATRICS, 2006.

HOFFMAN, GRETCHEN. *THE AMAZING HUMAN BODY: DIGESTIVE SYSTEM.* TARRYTOWN, NY: MARSHALL CAVENDISH, 2008.

HOLZMEISTER, LEA. *THE ULTIMATE CALORIE, CARB, AND FAT GRAM COUNTER.* ALEXANDRIA, VA: AMERICAN DIABETES ASSOCIATION, 2006.

JIMSERSON, M. N. *DISEASES AND DISORDERS: CHILDHOOD OBESITY.* CHICAGO, IL: LUCENT, 2008.

KIRBERGER, KIMBERLY. *NO BODY'S PERFECT: STORIES BY TEENS ABOUT BODY IMAGE, SELF-ACCEPTANCE, AND THE SEARCH FOR IDENTITY.* NEW YORK, NY: SCHOLASTIC, 2003.

LANCASTER, SCOTT, AND RADU TEODORESCU. *ATHLETIC FITNESS FOR KIDS.* CHAMPAIGN, IL: HUMAN KINETICS PUBLISHERS, 2007.

RINZLER, CAROL ANN. *NUTRITION FOR DUMMIES.* 4TH ED. HOBOKEN, NJ: WILEY, 2006.

OKIE, SUSAN. *FED UP! WINNING THE WAR AGAINST CHILDHOOD OBESITY.* WASHINGTON, DC: NATIONAL ACADEMIES PRESS, 2005.

POSKITT, ELIZABETH, AND LAUREL EDMUNDS. *MANAGEMENT OF CHILDHOOD OBESITY.* NEW YORK, NY: CAMBRIDGE, 2008.

TAYLOR-BUTLER, CHRISTINE. *TRUE BOOKS: THE DIGESTIVE SYSTEM.* DANBURY, CT: CHILDREN'S PRESS, 2008.

VELLA, MARK. *ANATOMY FOR STRENGTH AND FITNESS TRAINING: AN ILLUSTRATED GUIDE TO YOUR MUSCLES IN ACTION.* NEW YORK, NY: MCGRAW-HILL, 2006.

WEISS, HOWIE. *FUN, FITNESS, AND SKILLS: THE POWERFUL ORIGINAL GAMES APPROACH.* CHAMPAIGN, IL: HUMAN KINETICS PUBLISHERS, 2007.

WILLET, WALTER C., M.D., AND P. J. SKERRETT. *EAT, DRINK, AND BE HEALTHY: THE HARVARD MEDICAL SCHOOL GUIDE TO HEALTHY EATING.* NEW YORK, NY: FREE PRESS, 2005.

INDEX

ABOUT THE AUTHORS

DR. KIM CHILMAN-BLAIR IS A MEDICAL DOCTOR WITH TEN YEARS EXPERIENCE OF MEDICAL WRITING, AND A PASSION FOR PROVIDING MEDICAL INFORMATION THAT MAKES CHILDREN WANT TO LEARN.

JOHN TADDEO, FORMALLY OF MARVEL ENTERTAINMENT, IS A CELEBRATED COMIC BOOK WRITER AND DIRECTOR OF TWO AWARD-WINNING ANIMATED-SHORTS.